LOVE
MISCELLANY

To my
Valentine

LOVE MISCELLANY

EVERYTHING YOU ALWAYS WANTED TO KNOW ABOUT THE MANY WAYS WE CELEBRATE ROMANCE AND PASSION

DEBORAH A. LEVINE

WITH CONTRIBUTIONS FROM
KRISTIN KULSAVAGE

SKYHORSE PUBLISHING

With thanks to Laura Briskman.

Skyhorse Publishing books may be purchased in bulk at special discounts for sales promotion, corporate gifts, fund-raising, or educational purposes. Special editions can also be created to specifications. For details, contact the Special Sales Department, Skyhorse Publishing, 307 West 36th Street, 11th Floor, New York, NY 10018 or info@skyhorsepublishing.com.

Skyhorse® and Skyhorse Publishing® are registered trademarks of Skyhorse Publishing, Inc.®, a Delaware corporation.

Visit our website at www.skyhorsepublishing.com.

10 9 8 7 6 5 4 3 2 1

Library of Congress Cataloging-in-Publication Data is on file.

ISBN: 978-1-61608-386-1

Printed in China

For my mom and dad, who've shared fifty Valentine's Days and are still going strong. And for Ian, Lili, and Julian, my three great loves.

CONTENTS

Offerings

Modern Times

INTRODUCTION

My parents, who celebrated their fiftieth wedding anniversary this year, have never been prone to gratuitous public displays of affection (a peck on the lips is about as amorous as I've ever seen them get). They are, however, one of the most romantic couples I know, thanks in part to a Valentine's Day tradition they conceived of long before they collaborated on my sister and me. Each February 14, along with the requisite box of high-end chocolates or a new orchid for the garden (tropical flora trump roses for my neo-Floridian mom), my folks give each other cards—not one or two, mind you, more like five or six . . . each.

The cards my parents exchange are the standard store-bought variety. Some are funny, others sappy, all of them signed with decades-old pet names and oft-told in-jokes. For my mom and dad, the delivery is as integral a part of the tradition as the cards themselves. They don't simply hand them to each other in neat stacks on Valentine's morning. Instead, they stealthily tuck the cards into briefcases or lunch bags, under coffee mugs and atop key hooks. The idea is not for the cards to be challenging to find, more like surprising, in a familiar way, to discover. Just as through this annual ritual, my parents discover (or re-discover) the romance and affection that first sparked between them five decades ago.

In researching this book, I've learned an awful lot about love throughout the ages and around the globe that I'm willing to bet will be as new to most readers as it was to me. Who knew that the ubiquitous heart symbol we associate with love evolved from a stylized ivy leaf or that traditional Turkish weddings were celebrated for over a month? Who would have imagined that the Americans spend close to $350 million on chocolate—for Valentine's Day alone?

The most interesting bit of Love Miscellany I've discovered, the bit of knowledge that will stay with me even after the names and dates have faded, is that people everywhere, across the planet and throughout history, love to celebrate love. We're not content just to feel it or even to share it. We want to shout about it, show the world that we're lucky enough to experience it, and thank those who've allowed us to know it. That's what Valentine's Day is, and has always been, all about. For some, that celebration means a dozen roses and heart-shaped box of chocolates. For others it's a dedication on the radio, a midnight serenade, or a half-dozen cards hidden where they're sure to be found.

When it comes to celebrating Valentine's Day, birthdays or anniversaries in our house, my husband and I haven't exactly followed in my parents' sentimental footsteps. Like many of our peers, we've eschewed paper and ink cards for their digital progeny, e-cards, and buy heart-shaped goodies only for the kids. And yet, despite our lackluster celebrations, those special days tend to find us exchanging cutesier-than-normal e-mails and making eleventh-hour corner-store bouquet runs—indisputable evidence that beneath the unromantic veneer, we're grateful for (and needy of) these yearly reminders to recognize and celebrate that most coveted of all emotions: LOVE.

—**Deborah A. Levine**
Brooklyn, New York

LOVE
MISCELLANY

HOW WE
CELEBRATE LOVE

THE PATRON SAINT OF LOVE

DID ST. VALENTINE REALLY EXIST?

Valentine's Day was named for the Catholic Saint Valentine—that much is common knowledge. But who was this Saint Valentine, anyway? Perhaps a better question is "Who wasn't?" The Roman Martyrology, the Catholic Church's definitive list of saints, recognizes several different St. Valentines, at least three of whom were supposedly martyred on February 14.

Historical purists insist that few facts are known about any of the February Valentines, and none of them lead to romance. Most agree that one Valentine was a third-century Roman priest and another a bishop from Terni, both of whom were buried on Rome's Via Flaminia (though not in the same grave). The third Valentine lived and died in Africa, though the details of his life remain a mystery.

Did You Know?

Until the mid-twentieth century, Catholics honored the martyred saints each February 14 with the annual Feast of St. Valentine. So little information about any of them existed, however, that the observance was removed from the Catholic calendar in 1969. Nevertheless, feasts are still held by some Catholics who continue to follow earlier versions of the calendar.

Despite the dearth of historical information about the various St. Valentines, several persistent tales of their noble acts have been passed down through the centuries. Over time, the first two Valentines' stories have been so intertwined that there's no longer any distinction between them. Popular Valentine's Day legends most often have as the protagonist a single third-century Roman priest, who may have been based on either of them, neither, or both.

In one such legend, Valentine is martyred for refusing to follow a decree of Emperor Claudius II. Having decided that bachelors were better soldier material than husbands and fathers, Claudius passed a law forbidding young men to marry. Valentine, however, sympathized with the lovelorn young Romans, and, being a priest, secretly married grateful couples in spite of the law. When word of Valentine's clandestine side gig got back to Claudius, he was sentenced to death for his defiance and beheaded near the Flaminian Gate.

Did You Know?

At least three churches claim to house a portion of St. Valentine's remains: the Basilica of Santa Maria in Cosmedin, Rome (where his skull is displayed every February 14), the Church of Blessed St. John Duns Scotus in Glasgow, Scotland, and Whitefriar Street Church in Dublin, Ireland.

Perhaps the most popular tale of St. Valentine takes place while he's imprisoned (either for performing the illegal nuptials or, according to other legends, for aiding tortured Christian prisoners or attempting to convert the emperor to Christianity). The story has several versions, but all of them feature a young girl, often described as the jailer's daughter, who visits Valentine while he's behind bars. In one telling, the girl is blind, and Valentine miraculously restores her sight. In others, she offers him comfort, and he falls in love with her. The tale ends with

Valentine writing a letter to the girl on the eve of his death with the closing, "From your Valentine."

Whether or not a Roman priest was actually the author of the first Valentine's Day card remains unknown. If he chose to defend true love over the rule of the Emperor will always be a mystery. As with any tradition that's handed down over centuries, hard facts are ultimately beside the point. As long as his namesake day continues to be celebrated by sentimental humans, St. Valentine (whoever he was) will always be remembered as one of the original romantics.

Did You Know?

The fact that St. Valentine is the patron saint of love, lovers, marriage, and the betrothed won't come as much of a surprise. But Valentine's heavenly duties don't end there. He's also the patron saint of the young, travelers, beekeepers, and greetings, and against epilepsy, fainting, and plagues.

WHEN IN ROME . . .
HOW DID VALENTINE'S DAY BECOME A CELEBRATION OF LOVE?

Since any evidence linking a saint named Valentine to an act of romance is tenuous at best, how did the day observed in his honor become inextricably linked to love? The exact reasons behind the evolution of Valentine's Day are the subject of scholarly debate, but most historians agree that the romantic holiday we currently celebrate is based on the fusion of two ancient traditions.

Before it became known as St. Valentine's Day, February 14 was the eve of the ancient Roman spring fertility and purification festival Lupercalia. Dedicated to the mythical founders of Rome, Romulus and Remus, the celebration was named for the mother wolf (*lupa*) that supposedly nursed the infant twins to health in a cave where the festival's opening ceremonies took place each year. To begin the rite, an order of priests called Luperci, or "brothers of the wolf," met at the cave to sacrifice two goats (for fertility) and a dog (for purification).

After the sacrificial feast, young Luperci fashioned themselves loincloths from the goats' hides and tore the remaining skins into bands, which they then dipped into the animals' blood. Clutching the bands, the priests raced through the streets of Rome, touching women and crops alike with the bloodstained hides. While being slapped with bloody goatskin may not sound like a party to a twenty-first-century woman, the young ladies of Rome believed the ritual would increase their fertility, stave off sterility, and bring easy pregnancies and births to those already expecting. As the Luperci ran through town, the women gathered outside, each eager for her turn to be blessed by the sacrificial blood.

According to some historians, though fervently denied by others, the Festival of Lupercalia included a second ceremony, which took the form of a lottery. After their goatskin flogging (and, one hopes, a bath) Rome's eligible bachelorettes were invited to drop their names into a large box or urn. A procession of unmarried men then lined up to choose the name of a random young woman from the urn. The resulting pairs, many of whom had never met, became coupled for the following year and often ended up marrying.

As Christianity grew, the Catholic Church set out to abolish Rome's popular pagan rituals. In doing so, church leaders realized they would face the least resistance if they "Christianized" rather than outlawed these celebrations. In approximately 496, Pope Galasius I banned the Festival of Lupercalia and in its place instituted a new holy day dedicated to St. Valentine on February 14. The former sacrificial feast was now held in honor of St. Valentine, and the lottery's urn was filled with the names of saints rather than romantic partners. Instead of entering into courtship, lucky lottery participants were now tasked with studying and following the example of their chosen saint throughout the coming year.

As Rome grew in power, its traditions and customs changed and spread. In medieval England and France, it was a popularly held belief that birds began their mating season in mid-February. Some historians

believe that with the influence of Roman culture, this notion became linked with the Catholic celebration of St. Valentine on February 14, adding to the day's romantic associations (and inspiring the coinage of the term "lovebirds").

Birds, particularly doves, who are said to mate for life, have been represented in Valentine's Day imagery ever since the two calendar events became linked. Geoffrey Chaucer, in his fourteenth-century poem "Parlement of Foules" ("Parliament of Fowls"), made the first literary connection between the two with the lines:

For this was on seynt Volantynys day
Whan euery bryd comyth there to chese his make.

["For this was on Saint Valentine's Day,
When every bird cometh there to choose his mate."]

Written in recognition of the first anniversary of King Richard II of England's engagement to Anne of Bohemia, the poem is cited as the first written reference to Valentine's Day as a celebration of love.

Did You Know?

Among the customs that invading Roman armies brought with them was the Lupercalia lottery. In medieval England, the lottery became a popular tradition on February 14, when the names of both unmarried women and men were put into a box from which matched pairs were drawn. The men then wore their valentines' names on their sleeves, inspiring the saying, "Wearing one's heart on one's sleeve."

Valentine's Day links to romance date back to the first half of the first millennium, but it wasn't until 1537 that it was declared an official holiday by King Henry VIII of England. Valentine's Day wasn't widely celebrated as a day of love until the 1600s, however, when exchanging tokens of affection and handwritten valentines became customary among lovers and even friends. As settlers traveled from Europe to America, they brought their

Valentine's Day traditions along with them. The invention of the printing press and the advent of mass production soon led to store shelves stocked with commercial Valentine's Day greetings each February, rendering the holiday impossible to ignore for romantics and cynics alike.

January 27, 1918

My love for you tonight is so deep and tender that it seems to be outside myself as well. I am fast shut up like a little lake in the embrace of some big mountains. If you were to climb up the mountains, you would see me down below, deep and shining— and quite fathomless, my dear. You might drop your heart into me and you'd never hear it touch bottom.

(From writer Katherine Mansfield to her husband and publisher, writer John Middleton Murray.)

3

THAT'S AMORE

HOW IS VALENTINE'S DAY CELEBRATED AROUND THE WORLD?

ere in the United States, Valentine's Day has been celebrated in much the same way since at least the middle of the last century. Lovers, spouses, family, friends, and the occasional secret admirer exchange cards, candy, roses, and expensive dinner invitations. Schoolchildren have parties in the classroom, while adults break out the good champagne, indulge in gourmet chocolates, and splurge on sparkly jewelry. But how is the day of love observed elsewhere? In many parts of the world, Valentine's Day is celebrated in much the same way as it in the United States and Britain, but some countries observe their own customs, or have added a bit of local flavor to ours.

Here are some of my favorites . . .

The Danish have several unique Valentine's Day customs, including the exchange of poetry and candy snowdrops. Traditionally, Danes exchanged valentines known as "lovers' cards" that were transparent until held up to the light, when they revealed an image of a man presenting a gift to his love. Another popular style of Danish valentine is the *gaekkebrev*, or "joking letter." On these whimsical love notes, the sender signs off using a code of dots rather than complete letters. If the recipient identifies the secret admirer by Easter, she (or he) is rewarded with a candy egg.

During Australia's gold rush in the mid-1800s, miners suddenly found their pockets heavy with gold and chose to spend large sums of it on valentines for their sweethearts. Like the lavishly decorated Victorian-era valentines of Britain and France, Australian valentines were heavily ornamented with satin and lace, as well as seashells, flowers, and perfume. The most ornate cards actually featured real hummingbirds and other exotic birds (after a visit to the taxidermist, of course).

While most of England exchanges candy and cards on Valentine's Day, citizens of Norfolk really get into the spirit of giving. Since the Victorian era, Valentine's Day has been a big event in Norfolk, inspiring nearly as much anticipation as Christmas, and at some points in history, even more. Like Santa, a mysterious gift-giver named Jack Valentine visits Norfolk each February 14, delivering presents for Valentines of all ages. Also known as Old Father or Old Mother Valentine, Jack leaves his gifts on doorsteps around town, rings each doorbell, then disappears into the mist before the lucky recipients can identify him. There's a little bit of Jack Valentine in many of the year-round residents of Norfolk, too. It's not unusual for locals to exchange gifts with friends and acquaintances on Valentine's Eve, play good-humored pranks on one another, and occasionally even share the love with everyone on their block.

In Slovenia, Valentine's Day is traditionally a celebration of spring, while St. Gregory's Day on March 12 is devoted to love. Under the influence of much of the rest of the world, however, in recent years, February 14 has become a day of romance in Slovenia as well. Still, proverbs such as "St. Valentine brings the key of roots" and "Valentine, first saint of spring" persist, and Valentine's Day is recognized as the commencement of the growing season.

On February 14 in Japan, the way to the heart is through the stomach—not with sushi, but chocolate. Two kinds of chocolate are gifted on Valentine's Day, *giri-choco* (or "obligation chocolate") for coworkers, friends and relatives, and

honmei-choco ("favorite chocolate") for sweethearts. In Japan, it's only the women who give out chocolates on February 14 (female friends are given a third variety, *tomo-choco*, or "friend chocolate"). Men get their chance a month later on March 14, or White Day (an occasion launched by the candy industry), when they give white chocolates to the women in their lives in return.

In Mexico, as in many South American countries, Valentine's Day is celebrated much the same way as in the United States and Great Britain. Often referred to as *El Día del Amor y la Amistad*, or "The Day of Love and Friendship," Valentine's Day in this part of the world is also an occasion to show gratitude and affection for friends.

Valentine's Day is known as *El Dia de los Enamorados*, or "Lovers' Day," in Chile, Argentina, and Bolivia, as well as in Ecuador, where the men take the day's meaning to heart. Along with roses, chocolates, and other romantic gifts, Ecuadorian men celebrate their Valentines with song, serenading them with late-night love ballads.

In many Latin and Central American countries, the game of *Amigo Secreto*, or "Secret Friend," is played

Did You Know?

In Japan, while *giri-choco* is inexpensive and widely available, *honmei-choco* are gourmet confections that are either homemade or bought from high-end shops. Japanese women make sure to give *giri-choco* to all of their male colleagues and associates, as it's considered embarrassing for a man not to receive chocolate on Valentine's Day. As a result, according to some estimates, more than 50 percent of chocolate sales in Japan occur during the weeks leading up to Valentine's Day.

around Valentine's Day. Much like the Secret Santa game popular at schools and workplaces in the United States at Christmastime, *Amigo Secreto* is a gift exchange party game. Each player drops his or her name into a bag and blindly chooses the name of another player, to whom he or she must give a gift. Parties are held where gifts are exchanged and the identity of each player's *amigo secreto* is revealed.

In Colombia and Peru, the Valentine's Day bouquets of choice are made up of native orchids rather than roses, though Colombia is the largest exporter of Valentine's Day flowers in the world. While Colombians traditionally celebrate *El Dia del Amor y la Amistad* in the fall, February 14 festivities have become increasingly popular in recent years.

In most parts of Spain, Valentine's Day is celebrated on February 14. But in Barcelona, *La Diada de Sant Jordi* on April 23 is real day of love. Also called *El Dia de la Rosa* ("The Day of the Rose") and *El Dia del Llibre* ("The Day of the Book"),

Did You Know?

The United States imports more flowers from Colombia than anywhere else in the world, comprising 78 percent of Colombia's total flower exports. Between February 1 and February 14, flowers are transported from Colombia to the United States on as many as thirty flights each day, on their way to 22,000 supermarkets and 15,000 flower stands around the country. More than 200,000 Colombians are employed to cultivate and harvest more than 3,700 acres of flowers to satisfy the demand for U.S. Valentine's Day orders.

St. George's Day honors the patron saint of Catelonia who, the story goes, slew a dragon and saved a princess. According to the legend, a rosebush grew from the dragon's blood, and St. George gave the roses to the princess. Inspired by St. George's chivalrous deed, a Rose Festival celebrating romance and gallantry has been held in Barcelona since the Middle Ages. As April 23 also marks the anniversary of the deaths of two famous authors, William Shakespeare and Miguel de Cervantes, in 1932 *El Dia de la Rosa* was reinvented with a literary twist. Ever since, when a man gives a woman a rose on St. George's Day, she returns the favor with a book. "A rose for love and a book forever," is the unofficial motto of *El Dia de la Rosa*, which results in the sale of roughly four million roses and 500,000 books in Catalonia each year.

Did You Know?

The world is full of Valentines. In the United States, there are towns called Valentine in Alabama, Arizona, Arkansas, Indiana, Louisiana, Minnesota, Montana, Nebraska, New Jersey, Ohio, South Carolina, Texas, and Virginia. Maryland has a Valentine Creek, and there's Valentines Beach in New York. There's even a Valentine, France; a Valentine, Uruguay; and a Valentine Island, Australia. Other popular cozily named towns include Romance, Cupid, Romeo, Candy, Diamond, Rose, Heart, and, of course, Love. (Source: Internet Accuracy Project, with research gathered from the U.S. Geological Survey's database of officially recognized U.S. place-names.)

An early British Valentine's Day ritual practiced by unmarried women involved pinning bay leaves to their pillows at the center and each corner. According to superstition, doing so inspired the maidens to dream of their future husbands. Some versions of this tradition included the women eating salted egg whites before dozing off as well!

In the UK, Valentine's Day customs include the traditional exchange of cards, gifts, and candy between friends and lovers—but the publishing industry gets in the spirit too. Each year on February 14, British magazines and tabloids run love poems and sonnets along with the usual news, weather, and celebrity sightings.

The traditional Romanian equivalent of Valentine's Day, celebrated on February 24, is called *Dragobete*. The occasion is named for a Romanian folk character and is a derivative of *dragoste*, which means "love." In recent years, many younger Romanians have begun celebrating Valentine's Day with much of the rest of the world on February 14, a move that, not surprisingly, has been controversial with nationalists and cultural purists who view Valentine's Day as artificial and overly commercial.

The Welsh tradition of carving love spoons goes back many centuries. In the sixteenth and seventeenth centuries (and possibly earlier) it was customary for a suitor to carve an ornate wooden spoon that incorporated symbols of his feelings and intentions.

Horseshoes foretold luck, bells signified marriage, a lock implied faithfulness, and a heart meant love. The spoons played a dual role in a couple's courtship, both as an expression of a man's devotion to his beloved and as a signal to her parents that he was a skilled craftsman who could support their daughter financially.

The Swedish have been celebrating Valentine's Day for a mere half-century, ever since it was established in the 1960s by the nation's flower industry. Valentine's Day isn't an official holiday in Sweden, but that hasn't hurt the country's flower or cosmetics producers, which experience their second biggest sales period of the year in the weeks leading up to Valentine's Day (the first is around Mother's Day).

In Finland, Valentine's Day began appearing on the calendar just over two decades ago, in the late 1980s. The occasion was marketed as a celebration of friends as well as lovers, so it's no wonder the Finns refer to it as *Ystävänpäivä*, or "Friendship Day." Primarily teens and younger adults exchange Valentine's Day gifts of cards, flowers, and candy among pals and paramours alike.

In Saudi Arabia, the sale of red roses, heart-shaped gifts, and anything in red wrapping paper is banned during the week leading up to Valentine's Day. The nation is governed by an Islamic theocracy that opposes the celebration of most non-Muslim holidays, particularly Valentine's Day, which is viewed as encouraging "immoral" relations among unmarried citizens. The anti–Valentine's Day regulations are enforced by the country's Commission for the Promotion of Virtue and Prevention of Vice, and newspapers feature ads promising punishment to anyone who doesn't comply with the ban. The law is no match for the power of love, however. Valentine's Day enthusiasts get around the regulations by buying their red and romance-themed merchandise a few weeks before the holiday or purchasing their goods on the black market, where a red rose that would normally sell for the equivalent of $1.30 can go for more than six times that much.

As in many other countries, Valentine's Day is celebrated in China with the exchange of cards, flowers, candy, and balloons. The Chinese calendar also includes a day of love several months later that long pre-dates Western Valentine's Day celebrations. *Qixi*, or "Double Seventh Day" (also known as "Night of Sevens" or "Seven Sisters Day"), originated as an explanation for the position of the stars Vega, in the constellation Lyra, and the Altair, in the constellation Aquila. According to legend, these two bright stars on opposite sides of the Milky Way represent a pair of immortal lovers who are allowed to meet only on the seventh day of the seventh month of the lunar calendar. Rather than exchanging romantic gifts, the Chinese celebrate *Qixi* by stargazing and wishing for their perfect match. In some parts of the country, women also participate in needlework competitions, in honor of the folktale's fairy princess, who was known as the Weaving Girl.

The Legend of the Cowherd and the Weaving Girl

The story begins as the seven daughters of the goddess of heaven are taking a dip in a river on a visit to Earth. A lonely cowherd named Niu Lang notices the girls and, egged on by his faithful prankster of an ox, decides to hide their clothes. The seventh (and most lovely) daughter is Zhi Nu, or "Weaving Girl," the fairy responsible for weaving the clouds. The sisters convince Zhi Nu to retrieve their clothing, and in the process she finds she must ask Niu Lang to return them.

Having seen Zhi Nu naked, Niu Lang is obliged to marry her. Despite their less-than-romantic meeting, the two fall deeply in love, live together happily for several years, and have two children. In time, however, the goddess of heaven grows angry with her daughter for marrying a mortal and remaining on Earth rather than weaving the clouds. The hoddess summons Zhi Nu back to heaven and orders her to remain there for eternity.

Alone on Earth with his two children and without Zhi Nu, Niu Lang is miserable. Seeing his master's pain, the ox, who has grown ill, tells Zhi Nu to end its life and use its hide to travel to the heavens and find Zhi Nu.

Reluctantly, Niu Lang does as he is told and fashions a carriage out of the ox's hide to carry him up to the heavens with his children.

Catching sight of Niu Lang on his journey, the goddess of heaven removes one of her hairpins and slashes a sparkling river in the sky be-tween Zhi Nu and Niu Lang, condemning the two lovers to live on separate sides of what we now know of as the Milky Way forever. Despite her rage, the goddess of heaven agrees to allow one concession to her daughter's happiness: Once a year on the seventh day of the seventh month, the magpies of Earth can fly to the heavens to form a bridge across the river so that Zhi Nu and Niu Lang can spend a single night together.

The two lovers permitted to reunite for just one night are represented by Vega, the brightest start in the constellation Lyra, in the east, and the Altair, the brightest star in the constellation Aquila in the west.

Chocolate-Covered Cherry
Mochi Honmei-Choco

1½ cups *mochiko* (Japanese sweet rice flour)
½ cup sugar
1½ cups water 1 tbsp plus 1 tsp corn syrup
1 tsp almond extract
Red food coloring
Cornstarch for dusting
10 maraschino cherries, rinsed and patted dry
½ cup semisweet chocolate chips
2 squares unsweetened chocolate, finely chopped

In a microwave-safe bowl, microwave chocolate chips and unsweetened chocolate on high for 30 seconds. Stir and heat for another 30 seconds, then mix. Repeat the steps until the chocolate is melted.

Dip the cherries in the melted chocolate until they're well coated. Place cherries on a plate lined with wax paper and freeze for 20 minutes. After 15 minutes, make the mochi by whisking together the *mochiko*, sugar, water, 1 tbsp corn syrup, and extract. Remove ½ cup of the *mochiko* mixture and tint it a desired shade of red or pink with the food coloring. Set aside.

Dust a clean work surface liberally with cornstarch and keep additional cornstarch handy for dusting. Spoon 1 tsp of corn syrup in a small bowl and keep it nearby.

In a medium saucepan, cook the uncolored *mochiko* mixture over low heat, stirring constantly, until the mixture pulls away from the sides of the pan. Spoon onto dusted work surface and, with a well-dusted rolling pin or well-dusted hands, carefully roll or pat the hot *mochi* to a ¼- to ½-inch thickness, depending on your preference.

From the rolled *mochi*, cut circles 2.5 times as big as the chocolate cherries. Place a well-chilled chocolate cherry in the center of each mochi circle. Quickly wrap the *mochi* circle around the cherry, pinching the bottom to seal it. If you have difficulty smoothing or sealing the bottom, add a drop of warm water to the base. If the *mochi* cools too much as you work, heat it in the microwave for 20–30 seconds. Place the finished *mochi* on a plate dusted with starch.

For the hearts, cut hearts instead of circles into the pink *mochi* dough. To decorate, attach the hearts to the finished *mochi* with a drop of corn syrup and drizzle with chocolate. Wrap some cherries in pink *mochi* and make white hearts for contrast. Sprinkle colored sugar onto leftover warm *mochi* and roll into balls. Arrange an assortment of *mochi* on a plate or in a small gift box.

Marcie's White Chocolate Raspberry Macarons

These tasty *macarons* just might earn you a French kiss . . .

3 large egg whites*

2 tbsp granulated sugar

1½ cups – 2 tbsp powdered sugar

1 cup almonds (slivered, blanched or sliced)

1 tbsp cherry pink powdered food coloring

OR

¼ cup Dutch-process cocoa powder

*For best results, use eggs whites that have been left
3–5 days in the refrigerator, loosely covered

In a stand mixer fitted with the whisk attachment, whip the egg whites until they foam (think bubble bath), then gradually add the sugar until you obtain a glossy meringue (think shaving cream). Do not overbeat your meringue or it will be too dry. Place the powdered sugar, almonds, and powdered color (or cocoa, for chocolate shells) in a food processor and give them a good pulse until the nuts are finely ground. Add the mixture to the meringue, give it a quick fold to break some of the air, then fold the mass carefully until you obtain a batter that falls back on itself after 10 seconds. Give quick strokes at first to break the mass and slow down. The whole process should not take more than fifty strokes. Test a small amount on a plate: If the top flattens on its own, the mixture is ready. If there is a small beak, give the batter a couple of turns.

Fill a pastry bag fitted with a plain tip (Ateco #807 or #809) with the batter and pipe small rounds (½ inches in diameter) onto baking sheets lined with parchment paper or silicone mats. Let the *macarons* sit for 30 minutes to an hour so the shells will harden slightly. In the meantime, preheat the oven to 280 degrees. When ready, bake for 15 to 20 minutes, depending on the *macarons'* size. Let cool.

Once baked, you can fill the *macarons* right away or store them in an airtight container for a few days either on a shelf or in the freezer. Do not refrigerate.

For the filling:

> 1½ cups white chocolate, broken into small chunks
> 1/2 cup heavy cream
> 1/3 cup high quality raspberry jam or preserves

Heat the cream until hot. Drop the chocolate and jam into the cream and stir until everything has melted and blended together. Let cool until firm enough to pipe or spoon onto the *macaron* shells.

ers at play, joyous and gay,
owding the bliss of a year in a day!

SAVE THE DATE

THE MANY WAYS COUPLES TIE THE KNOT ABROAD

There are thousands of ways we celebrate love on a daily basis from a kind word to a warm embrace or a soft kiss, but the ultimate celebration of love is committing yourself in matrimony to the one person you could never be without. The very phrase "to wed" is derived from the ancient Greek term "pledge." A wedding is exactly that, a union between two people who pledge to make a life together, no matter what their culture or where they tie the knot. Today's wedding traditions have evolved from thousands of years of social, cultural and religious practices and are often a blend of the old and the new. In wedding ceremonies in a cultural melting pot like the United States, it's easy to see the influence of matrimonial traditions from around the globe. Some are meant as blessings of prosperity, while others represent and celebrate true and enduring love.

THAILAND

Although traditions vary throughout Thailand, a Thai marriage is often performed in compliance with Buddhist tradition (though this does not

Preparations for a Thai Buddhist wedding ceremony

grant it a legal status). To guarantee a successful marriage, an astrologer is consulted to find an auspicious date for the wedding, and ceremonies include the exchange of *sinsod*, or a dowry. To ensure their happiness in matrimony, the couple can make merit, a charitable act that can mean inviting monks to their wedding (which ensures donations for the monks), or donating to the local temple. If the groom donates money in the name of the bride's parents, the gift serves the dual purpose of honoring her family.

One day prior to the actual marriage, the couple pays their respects to the bride's ancestors in a generally informal ceremony. The wedding itself begins early the next morning, and takes place in a private home. Monks chant and place a lit candle in a bowl of water, which they'll later use to bless the couple.

Pictured here is the altar where the groom and bride kneel to be blessed with water by an elder.

Thai bride holding a bouquet of plumeria, a flower native to Thailand

At last the celebration begins. The groom and his family form a procession carrying trays bearing *khan maak man*, or "items for engagement," to the family of the bride. The procession soon finds itself obstructed by a series of gates, and to pass through each the groom must present an envelope of money. It is traditional for the bride's family to tease him and scoff at the money he offers before letting him through. Once inside, the groom's family brings gifts for the bride's family and food for the ancestors who have passed.

At the ceremony, a senior elder stands before the kneeling couple. Using a white thread, he ties together the heads of bride and groom and pours holy water over their hands. The elder anoints the couple on their foreheads, and then it is the guests' turn to pour water over their hands. White threads linked to the wrists of the bride and groom are soaked with the water and then torn. Whoever is left with the longest thread is pronounced the one whose love is the deepest.

JAPAN

Japanese Cherry Blossom

Many Japanese weddings are performed in the Shinto tradition (as an alternative to Christian or Buddhist) in which the ceremony is held in a Shinto shrine. As a symbol of the bride's maiden status, her skin is painted completely white and she wears a white kimono. She will also wear a headdress in one of two styles: the *wataboshi*, a white hood, or the *tsunokakushi*, which is worn to hide her pride and "horns of jealousy."

Traditional wedding hairstyle of a bride at the Meji shrine

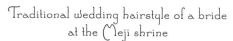

Japanese wedding procession

The bride and groom exchange vows, but it is the two families that face each other during this part of the ceremony. *San-san-kudo* follows, which is a three-times-three exchange of nuptial cups of sake involving the bride, groom, and their families. It is also traditional for the guests to drink sake as a means of contributing to the wedding bond.

At the wedding reception, everyone takes part in games and skits. The bride changes into a red kimono for the occasion, featuring a crane for long life. (Often, towards the end of the reception, the bride will change into yet another kimono.) Guests bring monetary gifts for the newlyweds, which are collected in a decorative envelope.

GREECE

A traditional Greek Orthodox marriage is seen as the uniting of the two families of the newlyweds, rather than simply the bride and groom. It begins with the celebration of the formal engagement—when the groom asks the father of the bride for her hand—and the

Red Geranium native to Greece

Newlyweds perform the money dance. Relatives and guests pin money to the couple as a gift. At some weddings the money is thrown in the air for the couple to catch.

wedding includes a full Greek Orthodox ceremony. It's customary for the *Koumbaros*, or the groom's best man, to accompany the couple to the church, where it's his job to assist the priest in leading the ceremony.

At the church, there is first a Service of Betrothal, an exchange of rings that the priest has blessed. Next is a Sacrament of Marriage, in which the couple is given burning candles. The *Koumbaros* then crowns them with *stefana*, or wreaths made of orange blossoms and linked by a silk ribbon. This crowning pronounces them king and queen for the day. After religious readings and wine, the couple makes three circles around the altar, in honor of the Holy Trinity. The *Koumbaros* removes the *stefana* and the couple is pronounced married.

The reception is very festive and is known for its *kaslamantiano*, or "circle dance," during which guests dance in two circles around the bride.

Church bells on the Greek isle of Santorini

The festivities also include guests breaking dishes for good luck, throwing money at the musicians, and drinking plenty of wine. Often, a pomegranate is broken on the ground to symbolize fertility and abundance and guests are given Jordan almonds as party favors. The almonds are distributed in odd numbers and are meant to represent the strength of the couple's bond, as they cannot be evenly divided.

IRELAND

The population of the Republic of Ireland is predominantly Catholic, so it's no surprise that most weddings involve a Catholic ceremony. But typical Irish weddings often include elements meant to inspire good fortune as well as faith. Many couples choose to be married on Saint Patrick's Day for good luck, for example, and a bride might carry lavender or a porcelain horseshoe in her bouquet for the same reason. Some brides also choose to braid their hair on their wedding day for luck, and as a symbol of feminine power.

Inside St. Patrick's Cathedral in Dublin, Ireland

As in many western countries, an Irish bride typically wears a white wedding gown. As she and the groom proceed down the street in the direction of the chapel, it is traditional for observers to bless them by throwing rice— and sometimes even pots and pans. The traditional Irish wedding ring is the Claddagh, which features two hands bearing a heart and topped with a crown. The hands symbolize friendship, the heart love and the crown loyalty.

Traditional Claddagh ring

It is believed that the concept of the honeymoon derived from the ancient Irish tradition known as *mi na meala*, or "the month of honey," when newlyweds traditionally drank honeyed wine together in seclusion during the first lunar month after their wedding. This was, presumably, to prevent their parents from trying to separate them. After one month one could believe that the bride had become pregnant and her marriage was considered secure. To honor this custom of *mi na meala*, Irish families typically offer newlyweds enough wine to last a month.

TURKEY

The family forms the core of Turkish culture, and weddings are major events. Traditional celebrations once continued for 40 days and 40 nights, but now last just three in rural areas and even less in cities, where typical ceremonies are similar to those in the U.S. Urban ceremonies typically take place in a rented hall or salon and sometimes a space reserved outside. The reception becomes distinctly Turkish when it's time to hit the dance floor. Guests at a Turkish wedding come prepared to dance the night away, the

The sun sets on the Blue Mosque in Istanbul, Turkey

Guests dancing in the streets for a wedding in Ankara, Turkey

men often performing traditional dances around the bride, at times locking knees and spinning in circles.

Rural Turkish weddings can vary greatly from region to region, each having specific traditions they celebrate over a three-day span. Most village weddings, however, are held in two parts: events for the groom's side, and those for the bride's side. The groom's events are the more public portion of the wedding, while the bride's events are held privately and are for women only. Most of the celebratory activities are held outdoors, thus weddings often take place in spring, summer, or early fall.

On day one of the celebration, the groom's side raises a Turkish flag to announce a wedding is taking place. At the time the flag is raised, a *kurban*, or sacrificial lamb, is butchered, to be served as part of a feast prepared for wedding guests. Endless glasses of aromatic tea are offered, and a delicious variety of foods are presented to guests. A band of musicians plays throughout the days-long festivities.

Day two is *Kina Gecesi*, or henna night, which is a celebration of the bride's last night as a single woman. For this ceremony the bride is dressed in purple or lavender stitched with gold thread, with a sheer red veil covering her head and face. The veils are ornate, decorated with tiny sequins or sparkling beads. A tray of henna balls with candles set in them is held over the bride's head while songs are sung. The groom's mother places a gold coin in the palm of the bride and covers it with henna. The bride's hand is then wrapped in gauze and a red mitten is tied over it. The guests adorn them-

Henna being applied to the bride's hands

selves in the remaining henna and enjoy an evening of dance and delicious food. At times, a belly dancer is invited to perform for the guests.

On the final day of a Turkish wedding, the groom's party sets out to retrieve the bride in cars decorated with streamers. The bride wears a white gown with a red ribbon tied at the waist and a red veil covering her face. Before she is presented to the groom's family, she's visited by some of the female guests who pin gold coins on her dress or slip gold bangles onto her wrists. When the bride arrives in the groom's village she is met by her husband-to-be and they lead a procession through the village that culminates at a table prepared for the ceremony.

In both village and city weddings, the bride and groom sit at this table where an *iman*, or official, performs the commitment ceremony. After the brief ceremony, the couple is pronounced married and a feast is served at the same table. The newlyweds are either greeted by guests at their table—where gold is pinned and placed on them—or the bride goes from table to table greeting the guests with a basket. Gold is seen as a more fitting gift than money because it holds its value well.

The tulip is the national flower of Turkey

AFRICA

Africa is a large continent with many diverse regions, each with their own religions, cultures, and traditions. Home to thousands of tribes, each tribe has its own wedding traditions that can be traced back several thousands of years. Wedding celebrations in this culturally diverse continent are often bright, festive occasions featuring rich colors, music and dance.

Traditional Moroccan weddings last up to seven days to allow for a number of pre-wedding ceremonies during which the families exchange gifts, furnish the couple's new home and purify the bride. This final ceremony is held on the wedding day itself, and involves

Moroccan newlyweds hold hands.

giving the bride a milk bath after which henna is applied to her hands and feet. The bride is then dressed in a traditional white-colored kaftan or a two-layered dress called a *Takchita*, and her eyes are decorated with kohl. Turkish brides typically wear a large headpiece with a veil and are extravagantly adorned in jewelry.

In South Africa, urban wedding attire combines both modern and traditional styles. Brides wear a white gown accented with colorful, ornate African shawls to represent their rich indigenous culture. Grooms wear dark suits with cummerbunds and bowties made from *kente* cloth. According-

ing to South African tradition, certain items should be used in the wedding to bring good luck, including honey, wheat, salt, pepper, water, wine, bitter herbs, a shield, a spear, a pot, a spoon, and a broom. These items stand for the twelve symbols of life, and represent the love and strength uniting the two families.

The Blue Cineraria is native to Africa

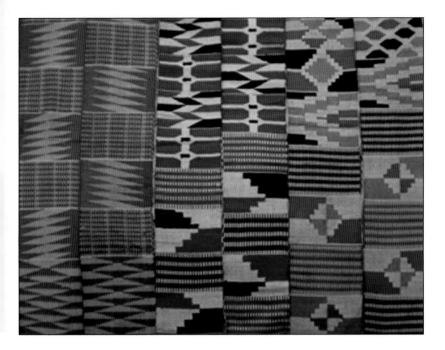

Kente cloth is woven from colorful strands of silk and cotton. Once the cloth of Kings, it is now reserved for important ceremonies and events. Both the patterns and colors hold special meanings.

In a traditional Sudanese wedding, seven broomsticks are burnt and disposed of to symbol the casting away of bad habits that can harm a marriage. The bride washes the groom's feet with water taken from an earthen jug, or *Kendi*, which symbolizes peace, and then breaks the *Kendi* before entering her new home. The bride then dines on a rice dish as a symbol of the last meal with her parents and a song is played during which the groom enters the home followed by the bride.

INDIA

Indian wedding traditions vary among both Muslim and Hindu religions, as well as the different Hindu castes. Many urban couples have ceremonies similar to those in the west, blending their past with modern trends.

Sweets, eggs, and money are tied to many wedding themes throughout India as they symbolize for the new couple a sweet life, fertility, and prosperity. Hindu wedding ceremonies typically include a ritual intended to ward off evil spirits from the new life journey the newlyweds are about to embark upon. After the wedding vows are exchanged, the family members of the bride and groom shower them with flower petals.

A traditional Indian bride wears a red or pink sari or *lehenga* on the day of her wedding, while the groom wears a turban. Once the bride is dripping

Hindu Indian wedding ceremony in a temple

in jewelry she is ready for the custom of putting *mehndi*, or henna, on her hands and feet. During the wedding reception, gifts are given to the new couple by dear friends and relatives.

Mehndi on the bride's hands

The Lotus is considered the flower of India

Romeo & Juliet

History and literature tells us that a romance is only as passionate as the lengths two lovers are willing to go to be with one another. The lesson these legendary love stories have at their core is that true love does not come without sacrifice. No star-crossed pair understood this better than William Shakespeare's Romeo and Juliet.

Shakespeare's tragic play follows two teenage lovers whose untimely deaths unite their feuding families. Set in Italy, the story begins with the Prince of Verona intervening between the two families of Capulet and Montague, promising death if there is a further breach of the peace. Romeo and Juliet first meet and fall in love at the Capulets' ball, unknowingly offering their hearts to the enemy. After the ball, in the storied "balcony scene," Romeo sneaks into the Capulet courtyard and the two lovers vow to marry despite their differences. With the help of Friar Laurence, who hopes the marriage will reconcile the two families, they are secretly married the next day.

Juliet sits at her balcony pining for her Romeo

Unbeknownst to the happy couple, their marriage night is the last they will ever spend in each other's arms. A series of unfortunate tragedies leads to the final heart-wrenching scene in which a sleeping Juliet is believed to be dead by Romeo. Shortly after he drinks a poison to join her even in death, Juliet wakes. Devastated to find her lover has died, and Juliet takes Romeo's dagger and ends her own life.

Written in 1595, Romeo and Juliet continues to enthrall readers and audiences today. Shakespeare's original script about two teens who truly loved each other more than life itself has been adapted numerous times over the centuries for stage, film, musical and opera.

SYMBOLS OF LOVE

5

To my Love.

SHOOT THAT GOLDEN ARROW

WHO WAS CUPID (AND WHATS WITH THE DIAPER)?

Each year as Valentine's Day approaches, we become reacquainted with Cupid, that arrow-slinging baby with a pair of snow-white wings and a diaper to match. But who is Cupid, really, beneath the blond curls and baby fat?

His image has evolved to that of the rosy-cheeked cherub, but Cupid, whose name is derived from the Latin *cupida*, or "desire," was originally a god of Greek and Roman mythology. The winged and, as the story goes, stunningly handsome son of Venus was known as Eros to the Greeks and had a reputation for being a bit of a prankster. With his quiver of golden arrows, Cupid's godly duty was to cause the creatures of Earth to fall in love and marry (or at least procreate).

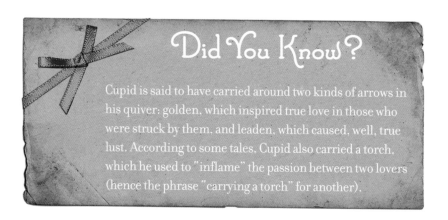

Did You Know?

Cupid is said to have carried around two kinds of arrows in his quiver: golden, which inspired true love in those who were struck by them, and leaden, which caused, well, true lust. According to some tales, Cupid also carried a torch, which he used to "inflame" the passion between two lovers (hence the phrase "carrying a torch" for another).

Cupid is probably best known for costarring in his own allegory, "The Tale of Cupid and Psyche," which first appeared in *The Golden Ass* by Lucius Apuleius in the second century AD. This legendary love story goes more or less like this:

Three daughters were born to a king and queen. Two were average looking at best, but the third, Psyche, was so beautiful, mere words failed to do her justice. Her beauty was so great that she was often compared to the goddess Venus (or Aphrodite, to the Greeks). Some even dared say Psyche was the more stunning of the two. That the very men who should be worshiping her were now heaping praise on a mere mortal did not go over

well with Venus. Furious, she ordered her son, Cupid, to avenge her by causing Psyche to fall in love with a wretch of Venus's choosing.

Cupid, despite his penchant for pranks, is ambivalent about his assignment, but agrees to go along with it in the end. When, having made himself invisible and flown through her window, he lays his eyes on the sleeping Psyche, Cupid finds himself feeling pity for the mortal who is too beautiful for her own good. While gazing at Psyche, Cupid accidentally awakens her, and she looks directly into his eyes, even though he is invisible. Startled, Cupid scratches himself, rather than Psyche, with his golden arrow, causing him to fall instantly and deeply in love with her.

No longer able to go through with his mother's plan, Cupid returns to Venus to explain what transpired. Outraged, Venus puts a curse on Psyche that prevents anyone, despite her beauty and charm, from

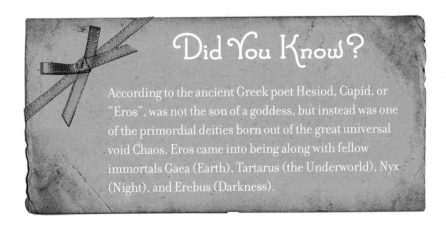

Did You Know?

According to the ancient Greek poet Hesiod, Cupid, or "Eros", was not the son of a goddess, but instead was one of the primordial deities born out of the great universal void Chaos. Eros came into being along with fellow immortals Gaea (Earth), Tartarus (the Underworld), Nyx (Night), and Erebus (Darkness).

falling in love with or marrying her. This angers Cupid, who refuses to shoot his golden arrows, putting an end to new love or life on Earth until Venus removes the curse.

Meanwhile, no matter how many compliments she receives on her beauty, Psyche remains alone while her two less-appealing sisters marry. In great distress, the king and queen discuss their predicament with the oracle of Apollo, who tells them that Psyche's destiny is not to marry a mortal, but a "monster" more powerful than either men or gods. The king and queen are devastated, but Psyche tells them no fate could be worse than her present lonely existence and insists she be taken to the top of the mountain as the oracle instructed. Once she is there, however, it is not a monster, but Zephyr, the west wind, who carries Psyche off and brings her to a spectacular palace nestled in a beautiful valley, where she is doted on by invisible servants.

By ceasing to shoot his golden arrows, Cupid makes his point to Venus, who reluctantly offers to grant him his wish if he resumes bringing love and new life to the planet. Cupid's one desire is Psyche, and so, when night falls in the palace, he visits her in her room and consummates their marriage.

For some time, the couple's days continue in this way—Psyche alone with the invisible servants by day, and Cupid swooping in just in time to spend the night. Psyche is gaga over her new husband but puzzled by the fact that he refuses to let her see what he looks like, insisting that she should love him for who he is rather than how he looks.

Happy but homesick, Psyche wants to show off her exquisite new digs to her sisters. Cupid consents, instructing Zephyr to bring Psyche's sisters to the palace for a visit—but not before warning Psyche to ignore them if they attempt to persuade her to find out his true identity. When her sisters arrive, Psyche shows them around the palace and, of course, they become extremely jealous of her new life. After some prodding, Psyche admits that she has never actually seen her lover, which gives her sisters the perfect opening to insinuate that there must be something wrong with him if he insists she cannot see him. They remind

Psyche of the oracle's prophecy that the husband who awaited her was a monster, not a god, and implore her to sneak a peek at him by lamplight one night just to be sure.

Psyche tries to do as Cupid tells her and put her sisters' suspicions out of her mind, but after more lonely days in the castle thinking of nothing else, she gives in to her curiosity. That night, as her sisters advised, with a lantern in one hand and a knife in the other, Psyche takes a good look at her husband as he sleeps. Much to her surprise (and relief), her true love is not the monster the oracle had spoken of, but the beautiful god of love, Cupid.

As Psyche leans over to get a better look at her handsome husband—or kiss him after pricking herself with an arrow and being overcome with desire, depending on which version of the myth you prefer—a drop of oil from her lamp falls on his shoulder and awakens him. Upon opening his eyes, Cupid meets Psyche's gaze for an instant and understands what has happened. Without uttering a word, he goes to the window, spreads his wings, and flys away. Devastated, Psyche tries to follow Cupid out the window but, being mortal, she falls to the ground. "Love cannot dwell with suspicion," Cupid calls out (among other things) to the sobbing Psyche as he flies off into the night.

When Psyche pulls herself together well enough to look around, she discovers that the palace and the valley have disappeared along with her husband, and she finds herself in a field near the city in which her sisters live. Psyche tells her sisters what transpired, which, of course, they find secretly thrilling, each of them inwardly scheming to become the next wife of the god of love. Whether Psyche tricks both sisters into believing Cupid has chosen each to be his new bride, or whether each

simply believe that with Psyche out of the picture it is now her destiny to become his wife is unclear. However, after Psyche's visit, each sister, in turn, journeys to the top of the mountain, believing Zephyr will carry her safely to Cupid's majestic palace. Instead, they fall from the peak to their deaths, never to be seen again.

With an aching heart (for her lover, not her sisters), Psyche continues searching for Cupid. When she comes upon a magnificent temple, she enters, hoping to find her husband there. Instead, she stumbles into a room in which grains of various kinds are strewn about. Unsure about what has happened, Psyche begins to sort the grains, inspiring pity in the temple's owner, Ceres. Hearing Psyche's tale, Ceres advises her to go directly to Venus and beg for her forgiveness. Psyche then visits the temple of Juno, who concurs.

Psyche takes this advice and makes her way to the temple of Venus. There, she implores Venus to forgive her and reunite her with Cupid. Enraged, Venus hurls insults at Psyche and accuses her of causing Cupid to fall ill from heartbreak and the burn from the oil lamp. Nevertheless, Venus agrees to allow Psyche to attempt three seemingly impossible tasks, confident there will be no way a mortal could succeed.

Psyche, too, is sure she will fail at the first task: separating grains in a basket. But a generous ant comes to her aid, rallying his army to help sort the grains and hiding when Venus returns to find the task miraculously completed. Ever more irate, Venus challenges Psyche to retrieve wool from a flock of golden sheep who are both protective and strong enough to kill her. When she reaches the field where the sheep graze, Psyche is visited by a river god, who explains how to safely gather the wool from the bark of a tree while the sheep sleep. Psyche's success at the second task causes Venus to seethe with anger. The goddess then instructs her to fetch water from a source protected by serpents and only reachable by gods. With the assistance of an eagle, Psyche succeeds at the third task, too.

In disbelief that Psyche could have achieved these feats on her own, Venus devises a fourth task for her would-be daughter-in-law. Venus is certain Psyche will fail at this final task, because to succeed she would have to defeat the curiosity and vanity that all mortals possess. To complete the task, Venus explains, Psyche must visit the underworld and fill a box with some of the beauty of Proserpina (or, to the Greeks, Persephone) and return it to Venus.

Believing death is the quickest way to the underworld, Psyche climbs to the top of a high tower and prepares to plunge. Before Psyche jumps, however, the tower speaks to her, explaining how to get to the underworld and advising her on how to appease the three-headed dog, Cerebus, and avoid other obstacles in her way. The tower also instructs Psyche not to be tempted by anything she might come across in the underworld, to eat nothing but dry bread while there, and, most important, not to open the box of Proserpina's beauty.

While in the underworld, Psyche heeds the tower's warnings and carefully follows its instructions for evading danger and avoiding temptations. Once back on Earth, however, Psyche is overcome with curiosity about the contents of the box. Feeling confident because she has survived her journey to the underworld, Psyche opens the box, intending to borrow just a bit of Prosperpina's beauty for herself. Instead, she releases a deep, cursed sleep that instantly envelops her.

Cupid, who has at last forgiven Psyche, can no longer stand to be apart from her. Taking leave of his mother's palace through an open window, he flies to Psyche's side, sweeps the sleep from her face, and replaces it in the box. With a gentle graze of his arrow, Cupid wakes Psyche and lovingly reprimands her for succumbing to her curious nature yet again. He sends Psyche to complete the task Venus had given her while he visits Mount Olympus to plead with Jupiter, the king of the gods (that's Zeus to the Greeks), to allow them to be together.

Cupid's star-crossed tale wins over Jupiter, who becomes so convinced Cupid and Psyche should marry that he calls a meeting of the council of the gods—Venus among them—to declare it. Mercury is then sent to fetch Psyche and bring her to Mount Olympus, where, upon arrival, she is given a cup of ambrosia by Jupiter and told to drink it for immortality.

At last Cupid and Psyche are united forever as husband and wife, lover and beloved. In short order, Psyche gives birth to a daughter, whom they name Voluptus, or "pleasure."

Marshmallow Cupids

To make each Cupid you'll need:

2 standard-sized marshmallows
2 miniature marshmallows
1 tbsp white frosting
1 circular cookie or cracker, halved
1 string of red licorice (3 inches)
1 tsp red decorating gel
3 red mini chocolate-coated candies (such as M&M'S)
1 tsp yellow sprinkles

Stack the standard-sized marshmallows to make the body, and secure with a dab of frosting. Once the frosting has dried, use more to attach the cookie halves to the back of the marshmallow stack for the wings and the miniature marshmallows to the sides for the arms.

Cut the licorice into two equal pieces, about 1½ inches each. To make the arrow, use small kitchen scissors to feather the end of one piece of licorice and use frosting to attach a small candy to the other end for the arrowhead. Carefully cut down the center of the remaining piece of licorice until the cut is ¼ inch away from the opposite end. Bend one side of the licorice strip to form the rounded side of the bow, and trim the other side to form the string. Slightly dampen the end of the "string" and press firmly into the bended bow. Attach the bow and arrow to Cupid with frosting.

To create Cupid's face, use frosting to attach two miniature candies of the same color for the eyes and use the red decorating gel to draw the mouth. Attach the sprinkles to the top of the head with frosting for the hair, and decorate the edges of the wings with gel.

Store in an airtight container at room temperature.

Spring 1919

Sweetheart,

Scott—there's nothing in all the world I want but you—and your precious love—All the material things are nothing. I'd just hate to live a sordid, colorless existence—because you'd soon love me less—and less—and I'd do anything—anything—to keep your heart for my own—I don't want to live—I want to love first, and live incidentally—Why don't you feel that I'm waiting—I'll come to you, Lover, when you're ready—Don't—don't ever think of the things you can't give me—You've trusted me with the dearest heart of all—and it's so damn much more than anybody else in all the world has ever had—

(Excerpted from a letter written by novelist Zelda Sayre to her soon-to-be husband, writer F. Scott Fitzgerald.)

6

I ♥ U
WHERE DID THE HEART
SYMBOL ORIGINATE?

When you hear the word "heart," what image immediately comes to mind? Chances are it's a pair of buxom red lobes that meet in a point and not a pulsing bluish-purple organ. Since the beginning of civilization, the heart has been considered the keeper not only of life but also of our deepest emotions, maybe even our souls. How did an anatomically inaccurate, almost cartoonish symbol come to universally represent this vital organ and the most coveted emotion associated with it—true love? Contrary to popular belief, the heart symbol owes more to botany than it does to biology.

Inspired by relics of ceramics created thousands of years before, ancient Greek and Roman artisans decorated their work with stylized depictions of ivy and other vines. Though a handful of pointed lobes protrude from true ivy leaves, these images were rendered with two rounded lobes at the stem and a single pointed tip. Stylized ivy leaves were frequently incorporated into pottery and paintings, particularly those of Dionysus, god of the vine, who embodied sensuality and passion. Hardy plants, able to survive in the harshest of environments, ivy vines were also depicted on

Greek and Roman gravestones as symbols of undying love. Similar images were carved into the graves of Christians, representing Jesus Christ, who was described as a "vine with an unselfish heart." According to historians, these early, stylized botanical images were the precursors of the modern heart symbol.

If ivy leaves are green, why then is the heart red? Scholars attribute this evolution to monks of the Middle Ages, who were known for their paintings of the Tree of Life.

Taking their cue from the ancients, the monks incorporated the stylized, double-lobed leaves into their artwork. It wasn't long before secular artists began "borrowing" this technique from the monks, introducing heart-shaped leaves into their paintings, including those depicting scenes of intimacy and love. Soon, artists began painting the leaves red, the color symbolic of blood, life, and love throughout history.

Eventually, the vines disappeared, and the heart-shaped leaf became simply the heart. Throughout Europe, the symbol began to appear on everything from paintings to watermarks to, eventually, playing cards. As Christianity spread, so did the icon. Religious art featured angels and saints offering their double-lobed hearts to God, and the Sacred Heart sect adopted the symbol as its logo.

Did You Know?

Some scholars have suggested that the heart symbol evolved from the seed of the Silphium plant, which has a very similar shape. Grown the ancient city of Cyrene (now in Libya), Silphium has been extinct for more than 2,000 years. In the seventh century BC, however, Silphium was popular in ancient Egypt as both a seasoning and a contraceptive. Silphium's connection to sexuality and passion is believed by some to have inspired the design of the symbol for love.

Did You Know?

In Buddhism, a similar heart symbol evolved from renderings of the leaves of the *bodhi* tree, or Holy Fig. Unlike the European symbol, the Buddhist icon represented enlightenment rather than love.

Even in medicine, the "playing card heart" was used to represent the anatomical heart. During the Middle Ages, the Christian church forbade tampering with the human body. Without autopsies, or even surgery, few medical practitioners ever laid their eyes on an actual human heart. By the thirteenth century, medicine had advanced significantly, but doctors continued to use the double-lobed symbol in their work for hundreds of years. It wasn't until the beginning of the sixteenth century that the great and anatomically faithful artist Leonardo da Vinci created an accurate rendering of the human heart.

By the Victorian era, the heart symbol had become integral to the design of the ornately decorated valentines in fashion at the time. Lace hearts were typically embellished with silk, beads, feathers, ribbons, sentimental rhymes, and images of Cupid, birds, lovers, or roses. Often the card itself would be cut in the shape of a heart, and special heart-shaped boxes were designed for the more heavily embellished or delicate valentines. Later, as Valentine's Day cards became less elaborate, the heart symbol persisted as the holiday's most recognizable icon. Heart-shaped candies, balloons, jewelry, and more fill store shelves in countries around the world each February 14.

These days, on Valentine's Day and every other, the ubiquitous heart symbol has become cultural shorthand for anything from true love to simply affection. In our correspondence, physical and virtual, signing off a note with a heart indicates fondness as often as passion. Ever since graphic designer Milton Glaser introduced his "I ♥ NY" logo in the 1970s, billions of T-shirts, bags, mugs, and bumper stickers have been produced touting Americans' ♥ for pretty much everything. We sport heart symbols on our clothing, our walls, and even our cell phone covers. And yet, next to the cross, the double-lobed heart is the most identifiable symbol on Earth. For millennia, it has represented the very core of our beings and our most deeply felt emotions. Sure, we're indiscriminate about using it to represent our feelings for everything from fishing to grandparents, but we have yet to come up with another icon that better represents love, in all its nuance, mystery, and glory.

Roasted Love Apple Soup

1 lb whole cherry tomatoes, washed
4 cloves of unpeeled garlic
4 tbsp olive oil
1 small onion, peeled and finely chopped
15 oz chicken or vegetable stock
Salt and freshly ground black pepper, to taste
Heavy cream, to finish
Chives, finely chopped, for topping
Heart-shaped croutons, for topping

Preheat the oven to 400 degrees. Arrange the tomatoes and garlic evenly in a large roasting pan and drizzle with 3 tbsp of olive oil. Roast for approximately 30 minutes or until the garlic is soft and the tomato skins begin to separate.

In a large saucepan, sauté the onions until just translucent, but not brown.

Remove the garlic from its skin and add to the onions. Add the roasted tomatoes and any juices from the pan. Add the stock and bring to a boil. Cover and simmer for 20 minutes.

Allow the mixture to cool and blend until very smooth. Sprinkle with salt, pepper, and chives and top with heart-shaped croutons. Stir in heavy cream to taste. Serve hot.

Chocolate Heart Soufflé

8 oz semisweet chocolate

4 oz butter

6 eggs

2–3 tbsp liqueur, such as Kahlúa or kirsch

4–6 small heart-shaped molds

Preheat oven to 400 degrees. Melt the chocolate and butter in the top half of a double boiler set over simmering water. Keep warm. In a separate double boiler, whisk eggs until warm. Remove eggs from double boiler, pour into mixer, and whip on high until the volume of eggs doubles. Remove the bowl from the mixer. With a spoon, fold the warm mixture of melted chocolate and butter into the eggs. Pour the batter into the pans, and place them into a rectangular baking pan. Create a water bath by carefully pouring in hot water to reach only halfway up the side of the soufflé pan, making sure no water spills over into the batter. Bake for about 20 minutes. Serve warm with whipped cream and fresh berries.

Sunday 19th

My beloved angel,

I am nearly mad about you, as much as one can be mad: I cannot bring together two ideas that you do not interpose yourself between them.

I can no longer think of anything but you. In spite of myself, my imagination carries me to you. I grasp you, I kiss you, I caress you, a thousand of the most amorous caresses take possession of me.

As for my heart, there you will always be—very much so. I have a delicious sense of you there. But my God, what is to become of me, if you have deprived me of my reason? This is a monomania which, this morning, terrifies me.

I rise up every moment saying to myself, "Come, I am going there!" Then I sit down again, moved by the sense of my obligations. There is a frightful conflict. This is not life. I have never before been like that. You have devoured everything.

I feel foolish and happy as soon as I think of you. I whirl round in a delicious dream in which in one instant I live a thousand years. What a horrible situation!

Overcome with love, feeling love in every pore, living only for love, and seeing oneself consumed by griefs, and caught in a thousand spiders' threads . . .

(Written in June, 1836 by the writer Honoré de Balzac to Polish countess Evelina Hanska.)

Raspberry Meringue Hearts

Whites from 3 large eggs, at room temperature

¼ tsp cream of tartar or cider vinegar

¾ cup granulated sugar

1 tsp raspberry extract

1/8 tsp red food coloring (liquid)

Confectioners' sugar

Parchment paper

2½-inch heart-shaped cookie cutter

Pastry bag fitted with a ½-inch plain tip

Position oven racks to divide the oven in thirds and preheat to 225 degrees. Line two large baking sheets with parchment, then, with the cookie cutter and a pencil, trace sixteen evenly spaced hearts on each piece of paper. Turn over the parchment so the tracings are facing down.

Beat egg whites with cream of tartar/cider vinegar in a large bowl with the mixer on medium speed until soft peaks form when the beaters are lifted. Gradually add sugar and beat on high for eight minutes or until stiff, glossy peaks form and the mixture no longer feels grainy. Beat in raspberry extract and food coloring until blended.

Spoon the mixture into the prepared pastry bag. Using the heart tracings as a guide, pipe the outline of the first heart. Continue to pipe concentric smaller hearts within the outline until the heart is completely filled with meringue. Repeat with the remainder of the hearts.

Bake two hours or until the meringues feel firm. Turn off the oven, but leave the meringues in for two more hours or overnight, until the tarts are crisp and dry. Peel off parchment.

To serve, arrange on a plate and dust lightly with confectioners' sugar.

You can make the meringues up to two weeks ahead and store in an airtight container at room temperature or in the freezer for up to two months.

Cleopatra & Marc Antony

This true love story about a powerful exotic queen and a Roman conqueror has captured the imagination of everyone from Shakespeare to Charlton Heston. Cleopatra was a seductive and charming queen who was a descendant of Alexander the Great and destined to be the last leader of the dynasty of Ptolemy I. A bold and determined leader who told her people she was a reincarnation of the goddess Isis, Cleopatra cemented her grip on the

Cleopatra

throne by marrying the Roman general Julius Caesar.

It was upon Caesar's death that Cleopatra met Marc Antony. Antony suspected Cleopatra was an accomplice in his murder and summoned her to Tarsus. There, the two formed an alliance and soon became lovers. Antony and Cleopatra returned to Alexandria for the winter, but when spring arrived they were forced apart due to civil strife in Rome between Antony's family and a man named Octavian. To restore peace, Antony returned home and entered into a loveless marriage with Octavian's sister.

Now allied, the Antony and Octavian embarked on military escapades to reclaim Roman territory that had been taken by rebels. Near the end of the campaign, however, Antony grew suspicious of Octavian's true motives

and feared his alliance laid elsewhere. Antony soon withdrew to Egypt to rejoin Cleopatra, who in his absence had bore him twins.

With Egypt's money and Cleopatra's blessing, Antony turned his back on Rome and waged war on Octavian. He also divided his lands amongst his Roman and Egyptian children,

Marc Antony

naming Caesarion, Cleopatra's son from her first marriage, as the legitimate and heir to Caesar's name. This action threatened Octavian, who had gained power, popularity and the loyalty by claiming to be Caesar's adopted son.

Back in Rome, Octavian's power grew. He began a war of propaganda against Antony in order to woo the traditional Republican aristocracy to his side. He argued that Antony had low morals because he left his faithful wife abandoned in Rome to be with the promiscuous queen of Egypt. His list of social crimes was long, the most reproachable being "going native," an unforgivable offense to the proud Romans. Antony fired back by claiming Octavian had forged his adoption papers linking him to Caesar. Antony was repeatedly summoned to Rome, but he chose to stay with his beautiful queen.

When the war began, Antony and Cleopatra's navy was quickly destroyed and the relentless Octavian trapped them by invading Egypt. There are several tales surrounding the tragic death of the two lovers. One poses that near the end of the war Antony was told Cleopatra had killed herself, and so he threw himself upon his sword. Upon learning he had been told a lie, Antony was brought to the monument in which Cleopatra was hiding to die in her arms. According to another version, Antony was killed by an Egyptian priest who favored Octavian and a captive Cleopatra was permitted to conduct his burial rites. When Cleopatra realized she was instead going to be paraded through the streets of Rome in Octavian's triumph, she took her own life out of pride. Either way, the tumultuous romance of Antony and Cleopatra had a decidedly unhappy ending.

Cleopatra mourning the loss of her Antony

HAND IN GLOVE

WHY IS THE GLOVE A SYMBOL OF LOVE?

Now merely an oft-misplaced cold-weather accessory, gloves were once a fundamental element of a proper gentleman or lady's attire. Gloves were designed for specific occasions, and etiquette determined which gloves should be worn by whom, and when. Once wardrobe staples, by the mid-twentieth century, gloves had largely gone out of fashion, making appearances only at high-society functions and on the hands of style-making celebrities such as Michael Jackson and Madonna.

Did You Know?

Ever the romantic, William Shakespeare forever linked gloves with love in this line from *Romeo and Juliet:* "See, how she leans her cheek upon her hand! O that I were a glove upon that hand, that I might touch that cheek!"

The glove has long been a symbol of love and courtship, however. Back in the time of royal kingdoms, a knight would ask his lady for her glove to keep beneath his helmet during battle, promising to protect it with his life. In the sixteenth century, if a man sent a woman gloves, it was considered a marriage proposal. If she wore them, it meant she'd accepted.

In the late 1700s, it became customary for a gentleman to give gloves to his sweetheart as a Valentine's gift that she would later wear on Easter Sunday. Ladies eager to receive a pair let their Valentines know by reciting the verse:

"Good-morrow Valentine, I go today;
To wear for you, what you must pay;
A pair of gloves next Easter Day."

Gloves remained popular Valentine's Day icons into the Victorian era. Men continued to gift the objects of their desire with cloth gloves, but paper replicas eventually replaced this trend. Included with the gloves or glove-adorned cards would often be the sentiment:

"If that from Glove you take the letter G,
Then Glove is Love and that I send to thee."

Did You Know?

Although wearing the gloves she'd been sent by her suitor indicated a woman's acceptance of his proposal, a mitten signified that the rejected gentleman should lose all hope.

Glove Cookies

Valentines of all ages will say "I do" to these spiced sugar cookies . . . and if you want to have fun, throw some mittens into the mix.

½ cup butter or shortening
½ cup sugar
1 tsp baking soda
1 tsp ground ginger
½ tsp ground cloves
½ tsp cinnamon
½ cup molasses
1 egg
2½ cups all-purpose flour
Sprinkles or miniature candies (optional)

With an electric mixer, beat the shortening in a large bowl on medium to high speed for 30 seconds. Add the sugar, baking soda, ginger, cinnamon, and cloves and beat until combined. Beat in the egg and molasses until combined. Add the flour, beating in as much as possible with the mixer on medium speed, scraping sides of bowl when necessary. Using a wooden spoon, stir in the leftover flour. Divide the dough into thirds, then cover and chill for approximately three hours or until the dough is easy to handle.

Using a floured rolling pin, roll one-third of the dough on a lightly greased cookie sheet until it's an even ¼ inch thick. Use glove cookie cutters (or make your own by tracing your hand on a heavy piece of cardboard and cutting it out) to make the cookies. Bake on a cookie sheet at 375 degrees until the cookies are firm and golden brown (about 10 minutes). Cool on the pan for 2 minutes, then remove cookies to a wire rack. Repeat with remaining dough, rerolling dough as necessary. Decorate with powdered-sugar icing, sprinkles, or miniature candy hearts (optional).

Powdered-Sugar Icing

In a small mixing bowl, stir together 2 cups of sifted powdered sugar and 2 tablespoons of milk. Add milk, 1 teaspoon at a time, until the icing is smooth and spreadable. For colored icing, divide the mixture into portions and add a few drops of food coloring to each.

To my
Valentine

FRILLS AND SPILLS
WHAT THE HECK IS A DOILY?

I f you grew up in the United States in the second half of the twentieth century, Valentine's Day meant three things: school parties, candy, and making cards out of lacy place mats —aka doilies—that seemed to exist for just one month each year. A doily is a small decorative napkin or mat that borrowed its name from a seventeenth-century dry-goods salesman named Doiley. In those days, doilies were typically woven from wool, although later versions were made of linen or cotton thread, crocheted, or knotted into lace. Among doilies' less glamorous functions was to protect valuable furniture from scratches when placed beneath vases, bowls, and other items of decor. Similar to the doily, but decidedly more exotic, was the lace handkerchief, the real precursor to the paper doilies pasted onto homemade valentines by modern-day kids.

In Victorian times, ladies would carry lace handkerchiefs with them in case they should need them as a prop for flirtation. In those days, it was considered improper for a lady to speak to a gentleman she didn't know, thus mutually understood rules for flirtation were a necessity. Etiquette dictated that if a lady found herself in the vicinity of a gentleman she fancied, she would drop her lace handkerchief on the ground as a signal for him to pick it up and return it to her. From there, the exchange of words was permitted, and the two moved on to the next step in the courtship ritual.

As a symbol of romance, the lace handkerchief, or doily, became a staple of the ornate valentines of the time. With advances in printing technology and the advent of mass production,

embossed paper and paper lace soon replaced the more expensive and time-consuming cotton or linen lace, and thus the paper doily was born. Doilies of the Victorian era were more intricate and delicate than those commonly available today, but the concept remains the same.

Ring-of-Hearts Napkin Doilies

1. Start with prefolded square paper napkins of various sizes and Valentine's Day-inspired colors.
2. Turn one of the napkins so that the closed corner faces you.
3. Fold the right corner toward the left corner and flatten to form a triangle.
4. Next, fold left corner toward triangle's longest side and flatten to form a thinner triangle.
5. With sharp scissors, create the top half of a heart by cutting a rounded lobe from the widest part of the triangle.
6. To create the pointed tip of the heart, cut off the bottom of the triangle from left to right, leaving at least ¼ inch intact on right edge. (The left side of the triangle will be the center of the heart.)
7. Unfold to reveal a ring of identical connected hearts.
8. Repeat with napkins of a variety of colors and sizes.

Pure Affection's
sweetest token
Choicest hint
— of —
Love Inspired
To my
Valentine

According to some historians, crocheted doilies and lace handkerchiefs were not the only predecessors of the paper doily. *Scherenschnitte*, the art of intricate paper cutting, was popular in Germany and Switzerland of old; it was imported by the settlers to

America in the late seventeenth century. Among the designs typical of *Scherenschnitte* were hearts, flowers, and birds, and the paper cuttings themselves were meant to express the displayer's faith. In time, men began to use *Scherenschnitte* to show their love for their wives and sweethearts as well in the form of cards that included sentimental verses and prose. Collectors and fans of *Scherenschnitte* believe these cards to be an early form of the valentine, and the elegant paper cuttings bear a strong resemblance to artfully crafted versions of the doily.

Scherenschnitte Hearts

1. Fold a sheet of paper in half and draw the outline of one lobe of the heart. Inside the lobe, create a pattern of smaller hearts and other shapes. If you wish, you can add rounded loops around the outer edge of the heart, but be sure to draw both the inside and outside of the loops, or you won't be able to see the heart shape beneath when you cut. Remember, anything you draw will be duplicated on the other lobe of the heart. If you want hearts or other shapes along the centerline, only draw one lobe or one side of the shapes.

2. Carefully cut along the lines of the image with sharp scissors. For more intricate designs, lay the paper on a cutting board or a piece of thick cardboard and cut out your design with a swivel-tip craft knife.

3. When you've finished cutting, remove the cut pieces and open the paper like a greeting card to reveal the design. To mount your work, paste your Scherenschnitte to a piece of colored paper to highlight the design. For a valentine, affix your design to a piece of folded paper and inscribe a romantic verse inside.

Art reprinted with permission from www.littleacorn.typepad.com.

To Fanny Brawne:

I cannot exist without you—I am forgetful of every thing but seeing you again—my life seems to stop there—I see no further. You have absorb'd me.

I have a sensation at the present moment as though I were dissolving. . . . I have been astonished that men could die martyrs for religion—I have shudder'd at it—I shudder no more—I could be martyr'd for my religion— love is my religion—I could die for that—I could die for you. My creed is love and you are its only tenet—you have ravish'd me away by a power I cannot resist.

—John Keats

(Written by poet John Keats to his beloved Fanny Brawne, the girl next door. Though the couple was secretly engaged, Keats had been diagnosed with tuberculosis before they met and died in 1821 at the age of twenty-five.)

9

FOR THE LOVE OF ROSES

WHY IS THIS BLOOM SO
POPULAR WITH PARAMOURS?

A h, the rose. Nothing says love quite like a single red blossom on a long, green stem or a dozen not-yet-open buds bound together in a bouquet. To most of us, the rose symbolizes love, romance, beauty, and grace, as it has to civilizations all over the world for thousands of years. But the rose is just one of hundreds of thousands of flowering plants on Earth. How did it alone become so iconic of love? The answer may have literally gone the way of the dinosaurs—believe it or not, scientists have found fossils of rosebushes millions of years old. We do know that roses were revered by nearly every ancient culture in the world, from the Egyptians who were entombed with the blossoms more than 5,000 years ago to the Chinese, who cultivated them with such verve that little fertile land remained to grow food.

Like St. Valentine himself, the significance of the rose as a symbol of romantic love is the stuff of legend. According to both Roman and Greek mythology, were it not for love there would be no rose. Numerous myths recount the creation of the coveted flower, all united by the notion that the rose was born of desire, longing, and passion. The most straightforward of these tales stars none other than the goddess of love herself. The first rose, it is said, was created when Aphrodite's tears mingled with the blood of her beloved, Adonis.

Another myth begins as Chloris, the Greek goddess of flowers, finds the body of a beautiful nymph in the woods and calls on her immortal friends to help her transform the poor creature into a flower. Aphrodite gives the flower beauty. The god of wine, Dionysus, pours nectar on the flower, creating her fragrant aroma. The Three Graces give the flower joy, charm, and brightness. When the gods finished bestowing their gifts on the flower, Zephyr, the west wind, stepped in, blowing away the

clouds so that the sun god, Apollo, could shine brightly upon her. The flower bloomed, more exquisite than any other, and was called the rose.

Greek Mythology also tells of Cybele, the earth goddess, who upon seeing the stunning goddesses Aphrodite and Athena, born of the sea and the head of Zeus, laments that she herself has never created anything so beautiful. Intent on outdoing the goddesses, Cybele creates a flower bud that so pleases the gods of Olympus that they water it with nectar. When the flower opens, the gods see that it's a thing of true beauty and dub the rose "The King of Flowers." (Later, in her poem "Ode to the Rose," Sappho referred to the blossom as "The Queen of Flowers," and the gender identification stuck.)

In yet another legend, a beautiful young maiden named Rhodanthe flees from the affections of her many eager suitors to the safety of the temple of Diana. Though they are friends, Diana grows envious that Rhodanthe is the object of so many men's desire. To make matters worse, the suitors destroy the gates to Diana's temple in the midst of their pursuit of Rhodanthe, infuriating her. Jealous and enraged, Diana transforms Rhodanthe into a rose and the men into its thorns.

According to the Romans, rosebushes haven't always had thorns. In one version of an ancient myth, playing in the garden as a child, Cupid tried to pick a rose, but discovered a bee among the petals, busy collecting pollen. The bee stung the young god of love, who headed straight for the arms of his mother, Venus. Angry with the bees, Venus removed their stingers and threw them into the rosebush, where they became thorns. In an alternate version of the myth, Cupid was already a young man when he smelled the rose and was stung by the bee. In anger, he shot his arrows into the bush, creating the thorns that would forevermore surround the beautiful flowers.

With so many legends surrounding the origin of roses, it's no wonder nearly every ancient civilization is described as having been "obsessed" by them. In the Middle East, Persians gave roses as gifts thousands of years ago, and the temples of Ur (now Iraq) are rumored to have been well stocked with urns full of coveted rosewater. The Egyptians literally took roses with them to their graves—many were buried with bouquets and garlands in their tombs.

Did You Know?

An old Arabic legend tells of a nightingale who fell madly in love with a rose. At the time, all roses were white, and nightingales hadn't yet learned to sing. According to the legend, the nightingale's love was so deep, he began to sing, and his need to be close to the rose was so strong that he pressed his body against it. The rose's thorns pierced through to the heart of the nightingale, and his blood turned the rose red for eternity.

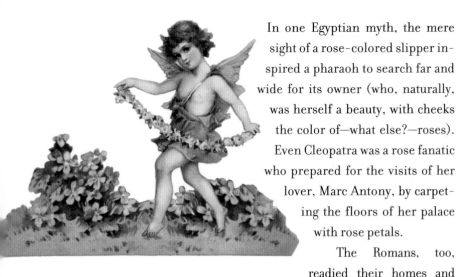

In one Egyptian myth, the mere sight of a rose-colored slipper inspired a pharaoh to search far and wide for its owner (who, naturally, was herself a beauty, with cheeks the color of—what else?—roses). Even Cleopatra was a rose fanatic who prepared for the visits of her lover, Marc Antony, by carpeting the floors of her palace with rose petals.

The Romans, too, readied their homes and banquet halls for feasts and celebrations by sprinkling the floors and sedans with rose petals. They adorned themselves with rose garlands around their necks, wore crowns of roses on their heads and literally ate, drank, and bathed in roses in one form or another. The rose was said to be the favorite flower of Venus, the goddess of love, and so too it became the favorite flower of all of Rome. In addition to love and beauty, the rose symbolized secrecy to the Romans. Roses hanging from a door or ceiling would indicate that anything said beneath them would not be repeated (hence the term "sub rosa").

With the fall of the Roman Empire and the rise of Christianity, the rose, though still a symbol of love and beauty, became a powerful religious

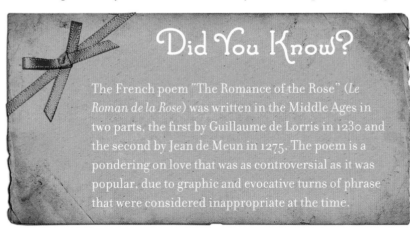

Did You Know?

The French poem "The Romance of the Rose" (*Le Roman de la Rose*) was written in the Middle Ages in two parts, the first by Guillaume de Lorris in 1230 and the second by Jean de Meun in 1275. The poem is a pondering on love that was as controversial as it was popular, due to graphic and evocative turns of phrase that were considered inappropriate at the time.

icon as well. In the years following the Empire's demise, the cultivation of roses continued in the East, but became too much of a luxury for anyone in war-torn Europe other than the wealthiest members of society. By the twelfth and thirteenth centuries, soldiers began returning from battle in the Middle East with stories of the magnificent gardens they'd plundered and seedlings or flowers they'd pilfered from them. Rose gardens began to return to Europe in the Middle Ages, along with the romantic notions they inspired.

Roses may have symbolized romance for millennia, but it wasn't until the eighteenth century that the giving of red roses became a sign of true love. In the early 1700s, the Turkish tradition of *selam*, or "The Language of Flowers," was imported to Europe from the East. *Selam* was a rhyme-based system, in which the names of flowers became associated with the human emotions they sounded like. (A contemporary English version, for example, might link "pansy" and "fancy.") When two unrelated European dignitaries brought home word of *selam*, a Western version was born. A century later, with the arrival of the Victorian era, the language of flowers had become all the rage in England, France, and eventually the United States.

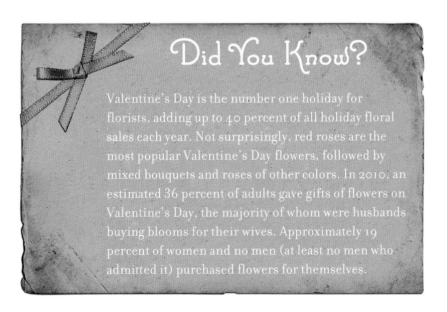

Did You Know?

Valentine's Day is the number one holiday for florists, adding up to 40 percent of all holiday floral sales each year. Not surprisingly, red roses are the most popular Valentine's Day flowers, followed by mixed bouquets and roses of other colors. In 2010, an estimated 36 percent of adults gave gifts of flowers on Valentine's Day, the majority of whom were husbands buying blooms for their wives. Approximately 19 percent of women and no men (at least no men who admitted it) purchased flowers for themselves.

At a time when being honest about one's feelings was considered too forward or coarse, the language of flowers, also known as floriography, was the only route to courtship for many young men and women. With the exchange of blossoms or bouquets, everything from an innocent crush to true love could remain unspoken and yet still be communicated. To be flirtatious, for example, a woman might "accidentally" drop a bunch of Sweet William near a man she admired. Offering a bouquet of sweet pea flowers, however, was as good as saying "It's over." By the mid-1800s, most members of society were well versed in floriography, and many relationships grew (and ended) by means of these coded conversations.

Did You Know?

Nosegays, or small bouquets of flowers, fisrst became popular in medieval times when sanitation was poor and having something sweet-smelling on hand was often a good idea. The term "nosegay" is actually quite literal: its pleasant aroma makes the nose gay or joyful. Other common names for the nosegay are the posy and the "Tussie-Mussie," a specific type of bouquet that uses the language of flowers to convey a specific message.

Did You Know?

Everyone knows a red rose signifies true love. But did you know a coral rose says desire? The rose has as many meanings as it does hues. Here are some of the more common ones:

Yellow = Friendship
White = Innocence/Secrecy
Pale Pink = Happiness
Dark Pink = Gratitude
Lavender = Enchantment
Black = Death

In the language of flowers, there are countless ways to express the nuances of infatuation, affection, and romance. Each floral variety *and* every color of blossom has its own unique meaning, but no flower says "I love you" like the rose. A rose without thorns means "love at first sight," a cabbage rose is the "ambassador of love," the moss rose is a "confession of love," and, of course, a red rose means "true love."

As the ornate valentines of the Victorian era faded in popularity in the early years of the twentieth century, so too did the language of flowers. With the coming of World War I, many would-be suitors were sent off to battle, and society's thoughts turned to more somber matters than decoding nosegays. Still, while few lovers today would suggest eloping with a bouquet of spider flowers, the rose has endured as an unequivocal symbol of love. If you want to say "I love you" to your special someone on Valentine's Day, she needn't know a thing about floriography. A dozen long-stemmed, just-on-the-verge of blossoming rosebuds will convey your message loud and clear.

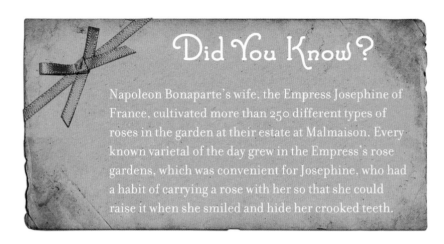

Did You Know?

Napoleon Bonaparte's wife, the Empress Josephine of France, cultivated more than 250 different types of roses in the garden at their estate at Malmaison. Every known varietal of the day grew in the Empress's rose gardens, which was convenient for Josephine, who had a habit of carrying a rose with her so that she could raise it when she smiled and hide her crooked teeth.

The Victorian Language of Flowers
(A Sampler)

Acacia = Secret love

Buttercup = Cheer

Pink camellia = Longing for you

Red carnation = My heart aches for you

Striped carnation = I can't

Coriander = Lust

Daffodil = Respect

Dandelion = A wish come true

Forget-Me-Not = True love

Forsythia = Anticipation

Gladiola = Love at first sight

Hibiscus = Delicate beauty

Purple hyacinth = Please forgive me

Iris = Faith and hope

Jonquil = Love me

Lavender = Devotion

White lily = Purity

Tiger lily = Wealth

Lime blossom = Conjugal love

Marigold = Comfort (or its opposite, pain)

Mistletoe = Kiss me

Oleander = Caution

Orchid = Refined beauty

Red poppy = Pleasure

Tea rose = I'll always remember

Snowdrop = Hope

Sunflower = Loyalty

Yellow tulip = Hopeless
love

Blue violet = I'll be true

Wilted flowers = Our love
is doomed

OFFERINGS

LOVE LETTERS
WHY DO WE EXCHANGE NOTES OF SWEET NOTHINGS?

For those who be-lieve an imprisoned third century Roman priest named Valentine wrote a letter to a young girl on the eve of his beheading with the closing, "From Your Valentine," sending love notes on February 14 is a tradition nearly as old as recorded history. Since no hard evidence exists of that event, however, let alone the girl or the note, most historians agree that the first "official" valentine was written hundreds of years later in the early fifteenth century.

Until the 1400s, sweethearts and would-be suitors, many of whom were illiterate, would share their Valentine's Day sentiments in speeches or song. While several early poetic and literary references to Valentine's Day exist, no examples of written valentines from that period have endured. In 1415, Charles, Duke of Orleans, was captured during the Battle of Agincourt and imprisoned in the Tower of London. While there, he passed the time writing love poems to his wife, which he then secretly arranged to be delivered to her. In one of the poems, Charles addressed his wife as his *doulce Valentinée*, or "gentle Valentine":

> "Je suis desja d'amour tanné,
> Ma tres doulce Valentinée . . ."
> ["I am already sick of love,
> My very gentle Valentine . . ."]

Considered the oldest written Valentine, Charles's letter is still in existence and is currently on display along with close to sixty others at London's British Museum.

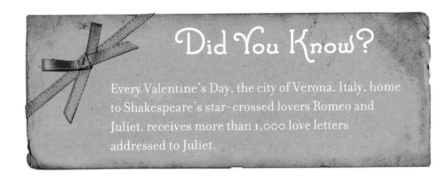

Did You Know?

Every Valentine's Day, the city of Verona, Italy, home to Shakespeare's star-crossed lovers Romeo and Juliet, receives more than 1,000 love letters addressed to Juliet.

Five years after the Duke of Orleans penned his famous poem, another poet named John Lydgate was hired to write a Valentine by Henry V, who played a key role in England's victory over France in the very same battle that led to Charles's imprisonment. The king commissioned Lydgate to write the poem for his fiancée, Catherine of Valois, as a Valentine's Day gift in 1420, the same year the pair would marry (giving Henry V reign over France along with his new bride). Lydgate, a young monk who was known to be a gifted writer, titled the poem "The Flower of Courtesy," and, like his role model Chaucer, included references to the mating of birds, as well as Cupid and St. Valentine.

It took a couple of centuries for Valentine's Day to embed itself into

European popular culture among all social classes. English and French literature of the fifteenth and sixteenth centuries includes frequent mentions of the occasion, but some believe the custom of sending Valentine's Day greetings can actually be traced to Germany. On New Year's Day, birthdays and other celebrations, Germans traditionally sent one another *Freundschaftkarten*, or "Friendship Cards." According to some historians, this custom made its way to France, England, and eventually the United States and evolved into what has become the modern tradition of exchanging valentines.

Handwritten valentines were *de rigueur* from the early 1600s until the late 1700s, when the convenience of commercial printing brought about the era of machine-made Valentine's Day cards. In the intervening years there were "Valentine Writers," books filled with romantic sentiments and verses that allowed even the least literate suitors to profess their love with ease. Along with words of woo, Valentine Writers contained decorative paper onto which the verses could be copied—some even included appropriate replies for recipients to jot down in return.

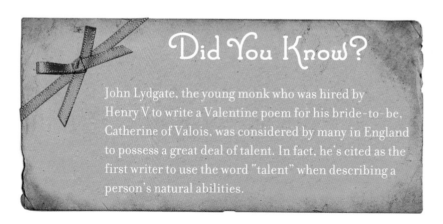

Did You Know?

John Lydgate, the young monk who was hired by Henry V to write a Valentine poem for his bride-to-be, Catherine of Valois, was considered by many in England to possess a great deal of talent. In fact, he's cited as the first writer to use the word "talent" when describing a person's natural abilities.

To My Sweetheart

Tell her that I love her—love her for those eyes,
Now soft with feeling, radiant with mirth,
Which, like a lake reflecting autumn skies,
Reveal two heavens here to us on earth.

Valentine:

If love's a crime, then I'm a rogue,
For all the passion's much in vogue;
Cupid's in fault, 'twas he that set,
Me thinking about thee my Bet,
Then punish him be easing me,
'Twill blunt the wanton's shaft he'll see;
Perhaps he'll promise ne'er again,
To give us honest mortals pain.

Answer:

For your passion I'm sorry, but don't be enrag'd
When I tell you in earnest I've been long engag'd,
Get what comfort you can, I assure you poor Ned,
It is Dick, and Dick only, shall share half my bed.

By the 1800s, store-bought Valentine's Day cards far surpassed hand-written cards in popularity. Improvements in the postal service in both

England and the United States made it possible for cards to arrive in a matter of days, rather than weeks, inspiring the exchange of more valentines than ever before on both sides of the Atlantic. Nineteenth-century Valentine's Day cards, particularly those made in France, were often elaborate creations, featuring frothy prose and poetry in intricately curling script and trimmed with ribbons, lace, and other decorations.

In the mid to late nineteenth century, Valentine innovators like the American Esther Howland and Britain's Kate Greenaway became renowned for their distinctive and sought-after designs. Such creativity came with a price tag, however, and the most ornate cards sold for as much as $5–$35. In the 1900s, large corporations such as Hallmark and American Greetings bought out smaller printing companies, ushering in the era of low-cost, mass-produced valentines. Even children could afford to buy Valentine's Day cards by the middle of the twentieth century, and class-

TO MY VALENTINE

I sure can make
good pie and cake
So please be mine
For "love's sweet
sake"

room valentine exchanges soon became an American tradition. According to greeting card industry statistics, children continue to send more Valentines than any other age-group.

Today, lovers, friends, and relatives send Valentine's Day greetings in a myriad of ways, both analog and digital. Around the globe each February 14, romantics both hopeless and hopeful continue to say "I love you" via every method of communications technology imaginable—e-mail, e-cards, instant messages, posts, tweets, texts, and whatever innovation comes next. But ink-and-paper cards haven't gone the way of the mix tape yet. According to American Greetings, more than one billion of them are sent annually, making Valentine's Day second only to Christmas as the biggest card-sending holiday of the year.

Did You Know?

According to Hallmark, more than half of all Valentine's Day cards purchased each year are bought in the six days leading up to the holiday. And that's not counting the e-cards the laziest among us remember to send on February 14!

November 2, 1856

*I already love in you your beauty, but I am only be-
ginning to love in you that which is eternal and ever
precious—your heart, your soul. Beauty one could
get to know and fall in love with in one hour and
cease to love it as speedily; but the soul one must
learn to know. Believe me, nothing on earth is given
without labour, even love, the most beautiful and
natural of feelings.*

*(From Russian writer Count Leo Tolstoy to bride-to-
be, Valeria Arsenev.)*

Napoleon & Josephine

Napolean crowning his queen Josephine

Joséphine de Beauharnais met Napoleon Bonaparte as "Rose." At the time, she had two children to support from her first marriage—her prior husband, Alexandre de Beauharnais, had died at the guillotine—and was still recovering from the shock of the Terror and her own close escape from execution. Napoleon rescued her from a life as a mistress and offered security for herself and her children. He also rechristened her, feeling that the name "Joséphine" was more fitting. The pair became

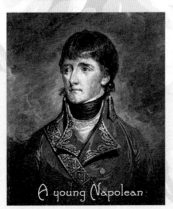
A young Napolean

lovers in 1795 and married in 1796. As a wedding present, Napoleon presented Joséphine with a gift emblematic of his confidence in their romantic bond: a gold medallion inscribed with the message, "To Destiny."

Unfortunately, Napoleon was forced to depart on his Italian campaign immediately following the wedding.

While there, he sent his new wife many love letters, asking her to join him in Italy, or even to write back to him more frequently. These pleas were to no avail, however, for Joséphine's interest had been caught by cavalry member Hippolyte Charles. Upon his return to Paris, a hapless Napoleon was to discover that Joséphine had not waited faithfully for him. To make matters worse, an angry letter on the matter written from Napoleon to his brother Joseph found its way into the hands of the London press.

Yet somehow, the two managed to overcome this scandal, at least in the public eye. Joséphine complied with her husband's wishes and became a loyal and tender companion and Napoleon took a few mistresses of his own in retaliation. Despite jealousy on both sides and the slow decline of their marriage's passion, the couple remained united by their bond. Joséphine provided a grounding source of peace for a man full of ambition.

While Napoleon was able to forgive his wife her unfaithfulness, the problem of an heir was a more serious one, however. When Napoleon impregnated one of his mistresses, he discovered that Joséphine was responsible for their childless marriage. Napoleon and Josephine were divorced in 1810, after which Napoleon let his broken heart mend and sought happiness elsewhere.

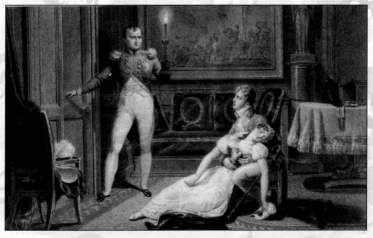

Josephine faints as Napoleon declares he wants a divorce

11

Entwining arms embrace love's charms,
Sweet lips the nectar taste,
There is no bliss like unto this,
When souls are interlaced.

HOW DO I LOVE THEE?

WHAT ARE SOME OF THE GREATEST LOVE QUOTES OF ALL TIME?

If you really want to make an impression this Valentine's Day, why not wow your one and only with a handwritten love note? To paraphrase Ogden Nash, candy is dandy, but a letter is better.

For inspiration, here are a few of the most famous lines about love . . .

"Love is comprised of one soul inhabiting two bodies."
—Aristotle

"One word frees us of all the weight and pain in life. That word is Love."
—Sophocles

"Love distills desire upon the eyes, love brings bewitching grace into the heart."
—Euripides

"What does love look like? It has the hands to help others. It has the feet to hasten to the poor and needy. It has eyes to see misery and want. It has the ears to hear the sighs and sorrows of men. That is what love looks like."
—Saint Augustine

"Being deeply loved by someone gives you strength, while loving someone deeply gives you courage."
—Lao Tzu

"My bounty is as boundless as the sea, My love as deep; the more I give to thee, The more I have, for both are infinite."
—William Shakespeare, *Romeo and Juliet*

"Love is like war, easy to begin but hard to end."

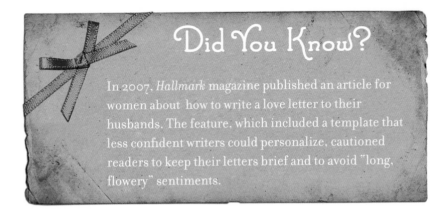

Did You Know?

In 2007, *Hallmark* magazine published an article for women about how to write a love letter to their husbands. The feature, which included a template that less confident writers could personalize, cautioned readers to keep their letters brief and to avoid "long, flowery" sentiments.

—Proverb

"Each moment of a happy lover's hour is worth an age of dull and common life."
—Aphra Behn

"I hold it true, whate'er befall;
I feel it, when I sorrow most;
'Tis better to have loved and lost
Than never to have loved at all."
—Alfred Tennyson

"Love is like quicksilver in the hand. Leave the fingers open and it stays. Clutch it, and it darts away."
—Dorothy Parker

"Take away love, and our earth is a tomb."
—Robert Browning

"Love doesn't make the world go round, love is what makes the ride worthwhile."
—Elizabeth Browning

"Come live with me and be my love, and we will some new pleasures prove, of golden sands, and crystal beaches, with silken lines and silver hooks . . ."
—John Donne

"But to see her was to love her, love but her, and love her forever."
—Robert Burns

"Thou art to me a delicious torment."
—Ralph Waldo Emerson

"Love makes your soul crawl out from its hiding place."
—Zora Neale Hurston

"I love her and that's the beginning of everything."
—F. Scott Fitzgerald

"In love there are two things: bodies and words."
—Joyce Carol Oates

"I love you without knowing how, or when, or from where. I love you straightforwardly, without complexities or pride; so I love you because I know no other way than this: where I does not exist nor you, so close that your hand on my chest is my hand, so close that your eyes close as I fall asleep."
—Pablo Neruda, "Love Sonnet XVII"

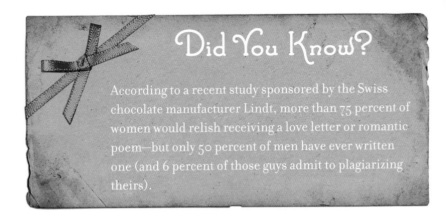

"You have to walk carefully in the beginning of love; the running across fields into your lover's arms can only come later when you're sure they won't laugh if you trip."

—Jonathan Carroll, *Outside the Dog Museum*

"I have learned not to worry about love; but to honor its coming with all my heart."
—Alice Walker

"Love is a temporary madness. It erupts like an earthquake and then subsides. And when it subsides you have to make a decision. You have to work out whether your roots have become so entwined together that it is inconceivable that you should ever part. Because this is what love is. Love is not breathlessness, it is not excitement, it is not the promulgation of promises of eternal passion. That is just being "in love" which any of us can convince ourselves we are. Love itself is what is left over when being in love has burned away, and this is both an art and a fortunate accident."
—St. Augustine

December 30, 1915

Off you go again alone and its with a very heavy heart I part from you. No more kisses and tender caresses for ever so long—I want to bury myself in you, hold you tight in my arms, make you feel the intense love of mine.

You are my very life Sweetheart, and every separation gives such endless heartache . . .

Goodbye my Angel, Husband of my heart I envy my flowers that will accompany you. I press you tightly to my breast, kiss every sweet place with tender love . . .

God bless and protect you, guard you from all harm, guide you safely and firmly into the new year. May it bring glory and sure peace, and the reward for all this war has cost you.

I gently press my lips to yours and try to forget everything, gazing into your lovely eyes—I lay on your precious breast, rested my tired head upon it still. This morning I tried to gain calm and strength for the separation. Goodbye wee one, Lovebird, Sunshine, Huzy mine, Own!

(Written by Tsarina Alexandra to her husband, Tsar Nicholas II of Russia, as the couple prepared to be separated by war.)

Rosewater Rice Pudding

1 cup basmati rice

4 cups boiling water

8 green cardamom pods

4 cups whole milk

¼ cup white sugar

2 tbsp rosewater

Salt

Crystallized rose petals for garnish (recipe follows)

Vanilla bean for garnish

Rinse the rice several times. In a bowl, add 4 cups of boiling water to the rinsed rice and soak for 20 minutes.

In a heavy saucepan, bring the milk to a slow simmer over low heat.

Drain the rice in a colander and add it to the milk mixture with a pinch of salt. Simmer over a very low flame for 30 to 40 minutes, stirring occasionally, until the milk has been absorbed and the rice is soft and chewy, but fully cooked.

Stir in the sugar, and taste. Add the rosewater one teaspoon at a time. Stir well and taste after each spoonful, adding more if necessary. When you can taste the flavor of the rosewater, but it's not overpowering, you've added enough.

Garnish with organic or pesticide-free rose petals or a whole vanilla bean, and serve warm or at room temperature.

Rose Petal Sorbet

2 cups milk
3 cups water
20 rose petals, washed
12 ounces sugar
2 tbsp rose petal water
Red or pink food coloring (optional)
Crystallized rose petals (recipe follows)

In a saucepan, bring milk and water to a boil and add rose petals. Let the petals infuse the liquid for about 10 minutes. Strain and add the sugar. Allow a few minutes to dissolve before adding the lemon juice and rose petal water.

Chill and blend in a sorbet maker. If you wish, add food coloring one drop at a time until you have the color you want. Garnish with crystallized rose petals

Crystallized Rose Petals

Rose petals, brushed clean
1 egg white, lightly beaten
Confectioners' sugar

With a clean, unused paintbrush, paint the entire surface of each rose petal with the egg white. Sprinkle the petals evenly with confectioners' sugar and space them out on a cake rack so that none are touching. When the petals have crystallized, place them on wax paper and use as soon as possible. Store in an airtight container in a cool, dry place (not in the refrigerator, where they will get soggy).

CARD CRAZY

WHEN WAS THE HEYDAY
OF THE VALENTINE?

In the eighteenth and early nineteenth centuries, handwritten valentines still ruled the day. But with the rise of the Victorian era in the mid-1800s, a new ornate style of valentine soon became all the rage in Europe and the United States. They were so in demand that they were produced in batches of tens of thousands. Despite this mass production, the cards featured an impressive level of detail and craftsmanship.

A die-pressing process was used to emboss the era's earliest valentines with intricate designs. The same dies were later used to create the paper lace that soon became a Victorian valentine staple. Multiple sheets of the paper lace were often layered to create a three-dimensional effect, aided by small pieces of paper with accordion folds that functioned as springs, elevating each layer above the next. Gilding and even gold leaf were used to decorate the lace, and "scraps"—small printed images depicting Cupid, flowers, birds, hearts, and arrows—were affixed to the lace before other embellishments were added.

Typical Victorian valentines were trimmed with ribbons, satin, chiffon, mirrors, dried flowers, feathers, beads, bits of fabric, spun glass, and more—often all at once. The most heavily adorned cards were too big and fragile to fit into standard envelopes and were packaged in their own boxes. Some cards featured mechanical elements that made the images depicted on the cards appear to move, dance, or fly. In addition to lace and frills, some valentines featured such novelties as miniature envelopes, mirrors, and slots for holding a lock of the sender's hair.

One style of novelty valentine that became particularly popular was the "Love Note." Designed to look like paper money, Love Notes were often imprinted with the logo of the "Bank of Love." One particular line of Love Notes looked so similar to actual British currency that printing was halted and exchange of the valentines was banned.

Other novelty valentines became trendy as well. Some of the most popular styles included . . .

The Cutout: Folded several times before small shapes were cut from the paper, these cards were like Valentine's Day-themed snowflakes.

The Acrostic: *The first letter of each line combined to spell the name of the recipient.*

The Flower-Cage or Cobweb: *The central feature of these cards was thin, intricately cut tissue paper with a piece of thread attached at the middle. When the thread was lifted, the paper took the form of a cage or web revealing a romantic image along with a Valentine's Day message beneath.*

The Beehive: *Like the Cobweb and Flower-Cage cards, Beehive valentines took on a third dimension when opened. For these cards, the tissue paper was folded rather than cut, forming a solid shape—often a heart—when fully revealed. Beehive table toppers and hanging decorations continue to be popular today for occasions and celebrations of all kinds.*

The Rebus: *These valentines included poems in which some of the words were replaced by pictures; For instance, an image of an eye took the place of the word "I."*

The Pinprick: *Using needles and pins, tiny holes were pricked into these valentines, creating the look of paper lace.*

The Religious: *These hand-cut paper lace cards were created by nuns and featured images of angels and the Sacred Heart. Some historians believe the heart symbol we associate with love originated as the Sacred Heart, and the cherubic depiction of Cupid so ubiquitous on valentines evolved from that of an angel.*

The Fraktur: *The intricate lettering of these valentines was similar to the style of lettering used in manuscripts of the Middle Ages.*

The Theorem: *Also called the "Poonah," they were made using a traditional Asian method of cutting stencils from oilpaper. The stencils were then painted over and removed, leaving behind the design on the cards.*

The Love Knot: *Sometimes paper, sometimes ribbon, the love knot was a symbol of enduring love with both Celtic and Middle Eastern origins. Like lovers intertwined, the knot's overlapping loops appeared to have no beginning and no end. Romantic verses were printed on the knot, so that the recipient would have to turn the card in her hands and follow the loops to read its message.*

The Proposal: *These valentines featured images of churches, wedding bands, or a bride and groom, often revealed when a partially detached "window" was opened. Many grooms-to-be waited until Valentine's Day to pop the question with a proposal valentine. In Britain, valentines designed to look like marriage licenses were also popular.*

The Pop-Up: *Toward the end of the Victorian era, pictorial cards that opened into a three-dimensional scene were in vogue. Some opened from right to left like traditional greeting cards, while others opened vertically or contained more than one flap that opened to reveal a "pop-up."*

The Puzzle Purse: As intricately folded as origami, these valentines included several verses that had to be read in order as the reader unfolded
the card.

Nancy's Puzzle Purse

In the olden days, valentine puzzle purses would often have the squares
numbered, to be read in order as each leaf is opened, with a final message
or picture in the center.

A puzzle purse is easy to recognize as it will have visible creases used to
fold it. Very often they were folded into thirds in both horizontal and vertical directions, with the resulting square then folded along its diagonals.
This results in the paper being divided into 9 equally sized squares, each
of which has an "X" mark, due to it having been folded along both diagonals. Traditional puzzle purses and baptismal certificates have invariably
used a folding method in which every one of the nine squares gains creases
on both diagonals, due to attempting to fold all squares at once. However,
this creates many creases unneeded by the puzzle purse.

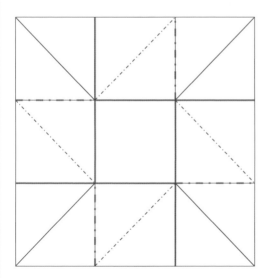

Without the extrane-
ous creases, the purse
will open and fold much
more easily, so it is best
to only fold along the colored lines shown. The two
colors are just used to aid
the eye. Dotted lines are
mountain folds (the paper

Directions to the Puzzle Purse reprinted with permission from Nancy Rosin.
Diagram illustration by Matthew L. Rosin. For more information, please see
www.victoriantreasury.com.

bends away from you) and solid lines are valley folds (you can look deep into the valley formed).

When finished, take two diagonally opposite corner squares, one in each hand. Fold the purple diagonal in each hand so you have two "ears," and bring towards center while twisting gently, bringing your right hand toward you and your left hand away from you so that the purse spins on its vertical axis. Flatten the pinwheel thus created, and fold each outthrust leaf across the center square in clockwise order. Tuck the last leaf into the center and you're done!

By the late nineteenth century, valentine designers began to take their cues from an increasingly popular style of Christmas card that was more pictorial than decorative. This new style of valentine was, quite literally, no-frills, featuring instead painterly images of traditional Valentine's Day symbols such as hearts, roses, Cupids, and birds. Pictorial valentines became an enduring trend and a precursor to the minimally adorned mass-produced cards that continue to fill stationery store shelves today. Still, it's hard to pass by a doily without recognizing the lasting influence of the Victorian valentine heyday.

Did You Know?

Special valentines were made for soldiers and their loved ones during the U.S. Civil War. Cards called "window valentines" depicted a tent with flaps that could open, uncovering a soldier inside. Other Civil War valentines included pockets for enclosing a lock of hair, images of men and women parting, or paper dolls with fabric dresses.

Valentine Fortune Cookies

2 large eggs, yolks discarded

½ tsp pure vanilla extract

½ tsp pure almond extract

3 tbsp vegetable oil

8 tbsp all-purpose flour

1½ tsp cornstarch

¼ tsp salt

8 tbsp granulated sugar

3 tsp water

Preheat oven to 300 degrees. In a medium bowl, lightly beat the egg whites, vanilla extract, almond extract, and vegetable oil until frothy, but not stiff. Sift the flour, cornstarch, salt, and sugar in a separate bowl and stir the water into the flour mixture. Add the flour mixture to the egg whites and stir until smooth, but not runny. The batter should drop easily off a wooden spoon.

Spoon level tablespoonfuls of the batter onto two greased 9 x 13 baking sheets, spacing cookies at least 3 inches apart. Gently tilt the baking sheet back and forth and from side to side so that each table-spoon of batter forms into a circle 4 inches in diameter. Bake 14–15 minutes, or until the outer ½ inch of each cookie turns golden brown and they're easy to remove from the baking sheet with a spatula.

While cookies are baking, write romantic fortunes on 3.5 x .5-inch slips of paper.

When cookies are baked, working quickly, remove each cookie with a spatula and flip it over in your hand. Place a fortune in the middle of a cookie and fold the cookie in half. Place the folded edge over the edge of a glass and bend both sides toward each other to form the fortune cookie shape. Store warm cookies in the cups of a muffin tin to keep their shape.

Love Knots

6 cups flour

6 eggs

1 cup sugar

½ tsp salt

½ cup vegetable shortening, melted

½ stick butter, melted

½ cup milk

1½ tsp vanilla or anise

½ orange, grated and juiced

Pour the flour into a large pan and form a well in the center. Mix together the remaining ingredients and pour into the center of the well. Mix until it takes on the consistency of bread dough. Knead well. Roll the dough into a ¼-inch rope, 4–5 inches long. Tie into knots and bake on a greased cookie sheet at 350 degrees until golden and very light. Sprinkle with confectioners' sugar or ice with a mixture of powdered sugar, milk, and lemon juice.

11 November, 1812

Write to me only once a week, so that your letter arrives on Sunday—for I cannot endure your daily letters, I am incapable of enduring them.

For instance, I answer one of your letters, then lie in bed in apparent calm, but my heart beats through my entire body and is conscious only of you. I belong to you; there is really no other way of expressing it, and that is not strong enough.

My health is only just good enough for myself alone, not good enough for marriage, let alone fatherhood. Yet when I read your letter, I feel I could overlook even what cannot possibly be overlooked. . . .

If only I had mailed Saturday's letter, in which I implored you never to write to me again, and in which I gave a similar promise. Oh God, what prevented me from sending that letter? All would be well. But is a peaceful solution possible now? Would it help if we wrote to each other only once a week?

No, if my suffering could be cured by such means it would not be serious. And already I foresee that I shan't be able to endure even the Sunday letters. And so, to compensate for Saturday's lost opportunity, I ask you with what energy remains to me at the end of this letter: If we value our lives, let us abandon it all . . .

(Excerpt from a letter by author Franz Kafka to the object of his desire, Felice Bauer. The two corresponded for five years, but never consummated their love affair.)

Elizabeth Bennett & Mr. Darcy

No couple better exemplifies a love-hate relationship than Mr. Darcy and Elizabeth Bennett, the quarrelsome lovers of Jane Austen's *Pride and Prejudice.* Their romance of frustration and, often, outright disdain, has captivated readers for generations.

Elizabeth and Mr. Darcy are the embodiments of prejudice and pride, and it is through many assumptions, misunderstandings, and stubbornness that their relationship almost never comes to be. Elizabeth, the headstrong second daughter of the Bennett family, and Mr. Darcy, a wealthy man whose façade of proud disdain is seemingly impenetrable, instantly dislike each other. Elizabeth's feelings remain unchanged, and she fails to not realize that her intelligence and personality have secretly captivated Mr. Darcy.

There has always been something captivating about the existence of a secret admirer, especially one you believed to be ignorant of your very

Mr. Darcy is invited to dance with Elizabeth

existence. Mr. Darcy's passionate love for Elizabeth, in spite of and because of her indifference to him, has inspired women to cry out for their own Mr. Darcys since the novel's publication in 1813. When Mr. Darcy finally reveals his love in an eloquent speech, his previous behavior looks begins to look like the teasing of a young boy pulling on the hair of a girl he likes. But when he qualifies his actions by telling Elizabeth that he fought against falling in love with her because of her circumstances (which were not quite posh enough), things go south. Despite Mr. Darcy's claim that his attempts to deny his feelings were fruitless, he doesn't get the girl.

After Mr. Darcy secretly saves Elizabeth's little sister from financial and social ruin, however, we come to the next part of every woman's daydream, in which the strong, stoic man has a soft, sensitive side that she is allowed to glimpse. As Elizabeth overcomes her prejudice and Mr. Darcy his pride, Elizabeth begins to fall in love with his honorable, gentle side. In true Victorian style, the two get married and move off to Mr. Darcy's considerable estate where they proceed to live a very British happily ever after.

Mr. Darcy converses with Elizabeth and Col. Fizwilliams as she plays the pianoforte.

13

THE HEART-SHAPED BOX
WHY DO WE GIVE CHOCOLATE TO OUR SWEETHEARTS?

When I was growing up, Valentine's Day meant one thing and one thing only: Godiva chocolates. February 14 was the one day each year our parents would splurge on my sister and me, at least in the gourmet candy department. My favorites were the cherry cordials, their syrupy red centers a luscious complement to the rich, dark chocolate coating. Truth be told, I would have devoured anything that came wrapped in one of those swanky gold boxes with matching elastic ribbon (as long as it didn't contain peanut butter . . . or insects). And the fact that I was given such luxurious treats on Valentine's Day alone made them that much sweeter.

Now you know how chocolates became synonymous with Valentine's Day for me, but what about the rest of the world? Cards have been exchanged for centuries, having evolved from the custom of sending handwritten notes. When in romantic history did chocolate become a symbol of love? Not so very long ago, as it turns out.

Until the late nineteenth century, sugar was heavily taxed on import, making it a luxury consumed primarily by the wealthy. When the tax was abolished in 1874, sugar became affordable to most Americans and Europeans. Over the next few decades, sugar consumption increased dramatically, and candies and sweets became popular gifts for a variety of occasions. In the 1890s, shopkeepers began selling heart-shaped satin boxes full of confections alongside their annual supply of Valentine's Day cards. By the early 1900s, heart-shaped boxes of candy—some weighing as much as five pounds—had become a Valentine's Day mainstay.

The first decade of the twentieth century proved that Americans were crazy about candy. By 1910, the nation had doubled its consumption of candy, spending $500 million on confections in that year alone. The sum is notable not only for its size but also for the fact that it doesn't include chocolate, as most Americans hadn't yet been introduced to the wonders of cacao beans.

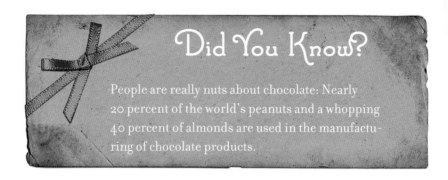

Chocolate, produced from the beans of the cacao tree, has been in existence for at least 2,000 years, probably more. The ancient Mayan and Aztec cultures in what's now Latin America both regarded chocolate with reverence and included its consumption in their spiritual rituals. In the cuisines to which chocolate is indigenous, the ground cacao beans are used in their unsweetened form, primarily as a seasoning or mixed into a beverage. The European explorers who first tasted chocolate on visits to the New World found it bitter and unpleasant. It wasn't until chocolate was imported to Spain, where it was sweetened with sugar and honey, that it became a popular drink in Europe.

Chocolate was consumed solely in its ground form until 1828, when a Dutch chemist named Conrad van Houten devised a way to separate the cacao butter and turn the rest into a powder that could be made into solid chocolate (by reintroducing a melted form of the cacao butter). Thanks to this invention, and other production innovations that followed, chocolate was no longer accessible to only the richest members of society, but available to almost everyone. In the late 1860s, Cadbury began selling boxed chocolates in England, and, thanks to the invention of Swiss confectioner Daniel Peter, Nestlé introduced milk chocolate soon after. In America, Milton S. Hershey created his first Hershey Bar in 1895, and within a few decades, the nation was hooked.

It wasn't until the end of World War II that the heart-shaped boxes crowding the shelves at Valentine's Day began to be filled with chocolates. During the war, soldiers were given chocolate bars as part of their rations,

and apparently they grew especially fond of the treats. In the years following the war, chocolates quickly became the most popular Valentine's Day confection. According to the National Confectioners Association, by the 1970s, 90 percent of all Valentine's Day candies sold were chocolates.

In recent years, with such a vast assortment of seasonal candies marketed at children to compete with, chocolates have slipped to a mere 75 percent of Valentine's Day candy sales. Not that that's small potatoes—in 2009, Americans spent more than $345 million on Valentine's chocolates, adding up to 58 million pounds of the stuff. With the media's seemingly nonstop touting of chocolate's nutritional benefits, thanks to its relatively high antioxidant content (present only in the ultradark varieties), there should be little concern that chocolates will go out of favor on Valentine's Day—or any other day—anytime soon.

What about chocolate's more sensual side? Claims of chocolate's aphrodisiac qualities date back to the days of the Aztecs, when Emperor Montezuma was reputed to feast on the beans before his many erotic escapades. Today, chocolate continues to be linked to romance more often than probably any other food, with the possible exception of oysters. So, is there any truth to these rumors, or are they just, well . . . rumors?

According to scientists, chocolate does, in fact, contain two chemicals that could hypothetically put one "in the mood": tryptophan, which helps make seratonin, a chemical in the brain that's linked to sexual arousal, and the stimulant phenylethylamine, which is present in our brains when we're in love. Chocolate also contains caffeine, another feel-good stimulant. Despite all the scientific evidence, researchers generally deny there's enough of any of these chemicals in chocolate to actually cause us to become aroused. What do scientists know about romance? Treat your valentine to some homemade chocolate liqueur or have a private fondue party for two, and do a little scientific research of your own. . . .

Spicy Hot Chocolate

Start your Valentine's Day with a little sugar and a lot of spice. . . .

5 oz high quality bittersweet or dark chocolate, coarsely chopped

¾ cup whole milk

½ tsp cayenne pepper

1 cinnamon stick (per cup)

Sugar

Combine milk, cream, and cayenne pepper in a small saucepan over medium heat and cook until simmering, about 4 minutes. Add chocolate and whisk until completely melted and well blended, about 2 minutes. Serve immediately with a cinnamon stick for stirring. Add sugar to taste.

Did You Know?

The average American eats at least a half a pound of chocolate each month.

Chocolate Truffles

8 oz good-quality dark chocolate (at least 70 percent cocoa),
broken into small pieces
1 cup whipping cream
3½ tbsp unsalted butter, diced and brought to room temperature
¼ heaping tsp instant coffee granules
Cocoa powder for dusting
Chopped hazelnuts or other nuts of your choice (optional)
Shaved coconut (optional)
Brandy or your favorite liqueur (optional)

Pour the cream into a saucepan and bring it to a boil. Pour the chocolate and coffee into a heatproof mixing bowl and slowly pour the boiling cream onto the mixture. (If you want to add brandy or liqueur to your truffles, now is the time to add a small amount.) Stir gently until all of the chocolate has melted, then leave to cool for approximately 2–3 minutes. Add the softened, diced butter and continue to stir gently. When the ganache has the consistency of mayonnaise, with no traces of oil on the surface, it's ready. Let the mixture cool for at least 3 hours in the refrigerator or, if possible, leave it overnight in a cool, airy room.

When the ganache has cooled, you're ready to form the truffles. Spoon a small amount of the mixture into a cool hand and shape into a ball of your desired size. Pour cocoa powder into a bowl and roll the chocolate balls in the powder until they're well dusted. To cover some of the truffles with finely chopped nuts or shaved coconut, simply skip the cocoa powder and roll the balls in the topping of your choice.

The truffles can be kept for up to three days. For a longer shelf life, dip the chocolate balls in melted chocolate before dusting them with cocoa powder or other toppings.

Chocolate Liqueur

This homemade liquor is delicious on its own, in an after-dinner drink, or added to coffee or hot chocolate.

1-liter bottle 151-proof rum
2 vanilla beans, split lengthwise
¼ cup cocoa nibs (find at gourmet and specialty shops or online)

Pour rum into a large bottle and add vanilla bean halves and cocoa nibs. Close the bottle and let it sit for at least three weeks, shaking bottle every day. Strain liqueur into a new bottle before serving.

The Valentine

Make this delectably indulgent cocktail with homemade chocolate liqueur and share it with *your* Valentine . . .

1/2 oz vodka
1/3 oz raspberry liqueur
1/3 oz chocolate liqueur
1/3 oz coffee liqueur

Pour the ingredients into a Collins glass, stir, and serve.

There would have been the making of an accomplished flirt in me, because my lucidity shows me each move of the game—but that, in the same instant, a reaction of contempt makes me sweep all the counters off the board and cry out:—"Take them all—I don't want to win—I want to lose everything to you!"

(From author Edith Wharton to journalist W. Morton Fullerton on June 8, 1908.)

10 January, 1846

Dear Robert Browning,

... Do you know, when you have told me to think of you, I have been feeling ashamed of thinking of you so much, of thinking of only you—which is too much, perhaps. Shall I tell you? It seems to me, to myself, that no man was ever before to any woman what you are to me—the fullness must be in proportion, you know, to the vacancy ... and only I know what was behind—the long wilderness without the blossoming rose ... and the capacity for happiness, like a black gaping hole, before this silver flooding. Is it wonderful that I should stand as in a dream, and disbelieve—not you—but my own fate?

Was ever any one taken suddenly from a lamp-less dun-geon and placed upon the pin-nacle of a mountain, without the head turning round and the heart turning faint, as mine do? And you love me more, you say? Shall I thank you or God? Both, indeed, and there is no possible return from me to either of you!

(Excerpt of letter from Elizabeth Barrett to Robert Browning. They married in secret on September 12, 1846.)

My Dearest Friend,

*... should I draw you the picture of my heart it
would be what I hope you would still love though it
contained nothing new. The early possession you
obtained there, and the absolute power you have
obtained over it, leaves not the smallest space unoc-
cupied.*

*I look back to the early days of our acquaintance and
friendship as to the days of love and innocence, and,
with an indescribable pleasure, I have seen near
a score of years roll over our heads with an affection heightened and improved by time, nor have the
dreary years of absence in the smallest degree effaced
from my mind the image of the dear untitled man to
whom I gave my heart.*

*(Abigail Adams to John Adams, her husband. He be-
came the second president of the United States. Written December 23, 1782.)*

CARNATION.
"...my own Carnation, sweetest flow'r I know",
Tho' of lowly station, dear, I want you so

14

THE WAY TO
THE HEART . . .
WHAT ARE APHRODISIACS
(AND DO THEY
REALLY WORK)?

I n simple terms, an aphrodisiac is anything that arouses sexual desire or improves sexual potency. As for the second part of the question—SPOILER ALERT—the short answer is, no. Humans have been searching for substances that enhance sexual powers for multiple millennia. With the exception of a hormone or two and a handful of traditional herbs, scientific research has so far failed to find conclusive evidence that any true aphrodisiacs exist.

So, why does the media inundate us with lists of the "Top 10 Aphrodisiacs" and "The Ultimate Aphrodisiac Menu" each year when Valentine's Day rolls around? Because a candlelit meal of sumptuous food and good wine with someone you love (or lust after) can be a genuine turn-on, science be damned. Like the placebo effect in medical trials, the power of suggestion is often enough to make people think they're more aroused or potent, even if, chemically, they're not. In fact, according to scientists and psychologists who study the subject, what we think may actually be the most powerful aphrodisiac of all.

If the researchers are right, then it's little surprise that many supposed aphrodisiacs gained their reputation based

Did You Know?

Herbs aren't just flavor enhancers. Chances are you have a cabinet full of alleged aphrodisiacs right in your kitchen. Almonds, anise, basil, coriander, fennel, garlic, ginger, honey, licorice root, mustard, nutmeg, and pine nuts have all been reputed to enhance sexual potency or pleasure.

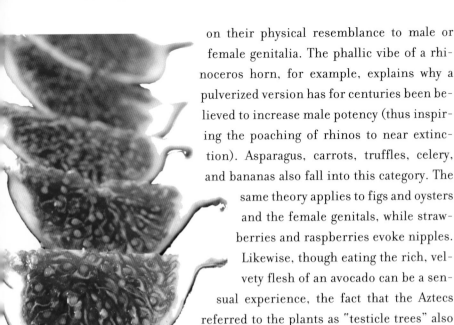

on their physical resemblance to male or female genitalia. The phallic vibe of a rhinoceros horn, for example, explains why a pulverized version has for centuries been believed to increase male potency (thus inspiring the poaching of rhinos to near extinction). Asparagus, carrots, truffles, celery, and bananas also fall into this category. The same theory applies to figs and oysters and the female genitals, while strawberries and raspberries evoke nipples. Likewise, though eating the rich, velvety flesh of an avocado can be a sensual experience, the fact that the Aztecs referred to the plants as "testicle trees" also contributed to the fruit's aphrodisiac lore.

Indulgences such as coffee, chocolate, and red wine may have no direct effect on our sex drive, but they can stimulate our senses, relax our minds, and lower our inhibitions. Other exotic edibles, like deer or tiger penises and Rocky Mountain oysters (buffalo or bull testicles), have long been rumored to have

Did You Know?

The scent of vanilla is said to inspire relaxation and pleasure (so much so that MRI facilities often infuse their treatment rooms with the aroma). Vanilla's aphrodisiac reputation has its roots in the Mexican legend of Xanat, the daughter of a fertility goddess who fell in love with a human. Banned from marrying a mortal, Xanat took the form of a vanilla orchid so she could remain close to her true love forever, providing happiness and pleasure for eternity.

aphrodisiac powers due to their presumably potent masculine origins. It's never been proven that ingesting another animal's sex organs enhances a human's ability to become aroused, but there are chemicals produced within our own bodies that, when supplemented, have been known to stir up the libido (testosterone), or increase our ability to experience pleasure (dopamine).

Did You Know?

Perhaps the most infamous and storied supposed aphrodisiac is Spanish fly. Also known as cantharides, Spanish fly is a powdered form of the dried carcasses of a species of iridescent green, southern European blister beetle with the scientific name Lytta vesicatoria. The substance is actually a poison that when ingested in small quantities and passed out of the body through urine causes an irritation of the urethra that results in a swelling and burning sensation that has been interpreted as sexual arousal. The line between the amount of Spanish fly that causes this sensation and the amount that can lead to irreparable damage to vital organs—and possibly death—however, is a thin one.

The Way to the Heart ...

Dark Chocolate Honey Almond Fondue

What could be sexier than feeding your lover luscious fruits dipped in an aphrodisiac cocktail of chocolate, honey, and almonds? Mmmmm ...

6 tbsp whipping cream

3 tbsp honey

7 oz semisweet or bittersweet chocolate, chopped

1 tbsp kirsch (cherry brandy)

¼ tsp almond extract

Assorted sensual fruits, such (strawberries, raspberries, banana and peach slices)

Candied ginger (optional)

Bring cream and honey to simmer in a heavy medium saucepan. Add chocolate and whisk until melted. Remove from heat. Whisk in kirsch and almond extract. Pour fondue into a bowl and place in the center of a platter. Surround the fondue bowl with fruit. For a little extra heat, add candied ginger for dipping. Serve with skewers.

Oysters with Champagne Ice

24 fresh, raw oysters
¼ cup shallots
¾ cup pickled ginger
½ cup dry champagne
½ cup sugar
2 tbsp fresh ground black pepper
¾ cup rice wine vinegar
1 tbsp chopped chives

In a food processer, combine shallots, ginger, champagne, sugar, pepper, and vinegar. Puree on medium-high for one minute. Pour mixture into a pie plate and freeze for several hours.

Clean and shuck the oysters, then place them on a serving platter. Just before serving, remove champagne mignonette from freezer and scrape one teaspoonful onto each oyster. Sprinkle each oyster with chopped chives and serve immediately.

White Asparagus with Truffle Vinaigrette

1½ lbs white asparagus, peeled and trimmed
1½ tbsp sherry vinegar
1½ tbsp fresh lemon juice
1 bottled black truffle (approx. 15g, 1 inch in diameter), finely minced
½ tsp kosher salt plus more for sprinkling
4½ tbsp hazelnut or walnut oil
1½ tbsp chicken broth or truffle liquid from bottle
Fresh chervil sprigs or chopped fresh chives for garnish

Steam asparagus over boiling water until tender, about 10 minutes.

Meanwhile, prepare the vinaigrette: Whisk together vinegar, lemon juice, minced truffle, and salt. Add fresh ground pepper to taste. Add oil in a slow stream, whisking. Whisk in broth, and season with more salt and pepper if necessary.

Using tongs, carefully transfer asparagus to a paper towel and pat dry. Arrange asparagus spears on plates and dress with vinaigrette. Sprinkle with herbs. Serve warm.

Avocado Gelato

2 cups whole milk

¾ cup sugar

3 strips fresh orange zest

2 tbsp cornstarch

Salt

2 California avocados, firm but ripe (1 to 1¼ lb)

Bring 1¾ cups milk, ½ cup sugar, zest, and a pinch of salt to a simmer in a 2-quart heavy saucepan over medium heat. In a small bowl, whisk cornstarch and remaining ¼ cup milk until smooth, then whisk into simmering milk. Bring to a boil, whisking constantly. Boil for one minute. Transfer mixture to a metal bowl, then set bowl in a larger bowl of ice and cold water and cool completely, stirring frequently. Discard zest.

Quarter, pit, and peel avocados, then purée until smooth in a food processor with remaining ¼ cup sugar. Add milk mixture and blend well. Freeze avocado mixture in an ice cream maker, then transfer to an airtight container and freeze until hardened, about 1 hour.

MODERN TIMES

15 MY HEART'S BEST LOVE.

BE MINE

WHO INVENTED
CONVERSATION HEARTS
CANDIES?

For many Americans, Valentine's Day is practically synonymous with Conversation Hearts, those ubiquitous pastel-colored candy hearts emblazoned with messages like "TRUE LOVE" and "COOL DUDE." Bags and boxes of the iconic confections begin filling pharmacy shelves in early January each year, replacing what's left of the season's marked-down Christmas candy. Despite their twenty-first-century sentiments, Conversation Hearts have been Valentine's Day favorites for nearly 150 years.

In the late 1840s, Bostonian Oliver Chase patented a machine called a "lozenge cutter," which was to become the first candy-making machine invented in America. With the cutter at the ready, Oliver and his brother Silas Edwin founded a candy-manufacturing corporation called Chase and Company. In 1864, a third Chase brother named Daniel packed up a Chase Lozenge Machine and headed west to Chicago to establish his own candy-making business.

Around the time Daniel Chase arrived in Chicago, a type of candy called "cockles" was popular in America. A crunchy confection of sugar and flour, cockles were shaped like scallops or clamshells and contained a rolled strip of paper imprinted with a short phrase or "motto." Inspired by the novelty of cockles, Daniel began experimenting with ways of printing mottos directly onto candies themselves. In 1866, Daniel's efforts paid off in the form of a machine that used a felt roller pad and vegetable coloring to stamp messages onto peppermint lozenges.

Did You Know?

If you lined up the 8 billion Conversation Hearts produced each year, they'd stretch 5,924 miles across the United States from coast to coast.

Daniel's "Conversation Candies" were a smashing success. Almost immediately, word of and demand for the clever confections spread from coast to coast. The lozenges weren't marketed for a specific holiday at first, but they quickly became favorite conversation starters at adult social gatherings. Special tongue-in-cheek mottos were printed for weddings, such as "Married in white, You have chosen right," and "Married in Pink, He will take to drink."

In 1871, just a few years after the debut of his enormously popular candies, Daniel Chase's factory was destroyed by the great Chicago Fire. Rather than rebuild, Daniel returned to Boston, where he was hired by the candy-makers Fobes, Hayward and Company to produce his Conversation Candies. Later, in 1902, the three largest confectionary firms, Chase & Company, Fobes, Hayward & Company and Wright & Moody, merged to form the New England Candy Company, or NECCO. The powerful new conglomerate was soon selling its products in every one of the United States as well as in England, all over Europe, and in Australia and South America.

In 1902, NECCO began producing the Sweethearts Conversation Hearts, originally called "Motto Hearts," that continue to be sold today. Along with the hearts, the company made lozenges in the shape of postcards, baseballs, horseshoes, watches, and more. At first, the candies

were larger than the dime-size hearts we're used to, in order to fit longer messages. But over time, both the mottos and the Sweethearts became more compact. In the 108 years since the first Conversation Hearts were pressed and stamped in the NECCO factory, over 250 billion more have been produced. And knock-offs have defnitely followed in NECCO's success.

In 1981, NECCO launched a line of Sweethearts with mottos in Spanish that were marketed to Latino communities in the United States and later nationwide.

With the exception of the Spanish-language version, the same Sweethearts mottos had endured year after year for decades, until the 1990s, when NECCO vice president Walter Marshall made the bold move to add a handful of new messages and say good-bye to some existing ones each year. Marshall's first new contribution, "FAX ME," was considered high-tech at the time, and was a big hit with consumers.

After over a century of producing Sweethearts with the same recipe (primarily sugar, corn syrup, colorings and flavorings), in 2010 NECCO introduced an entirely new kind of Conversation Heart (along with an iPhone app). The crisp texture, traditional flavors and pastel colors were replaced by brighter, bolder hues and fruitier flavors in a chewy formula. Along with changing their recipe, NECCO opted to retire its entire list of mottos and create new ones based on a competition among fans. Such twenty-

Did You Know?

In 2010, NECCO asked fans to vote on their favorite mottos, but the company takes requests any time: If a customer wants a particular message, they'll do a custom run for anyone willing to foot the bill for 1.6 million Sweethearts—as long as they're able to cart all 3,500 pounds of them home.

first-century innovations failed to impress some Sweethearts loyalists, though whether a return to the original recipe is in store remains to be seen.

What is certain is that Conversation Hearts are a force to be reckoned with in candy aisles everywhere. Production of each year's new batch begins just after Valentine's Day and continues into January of the following year. Eight billion hearts are produced annually, which translates to roughly 100,000 pounds of Sweethearts each day—all of which sell out in the six-week window between New Year's Day and Valentine's Day.

Did You Know?

The 2004 U.S. Love Stamp featured a pair of Conversation Hearts.

Cupid Says Game

Choose three or four each of all the Conversation Hearts with messages that work as responses to Yes or No questions, such as "Let It Be," "It's Love," "Yes, Dear," "I Do," "You Wish," etc. Put in a jar.

Think of a Yes or No question that you'd like to know the answer to, such as, "Will I fall in love this year?" Say your question aloud (or to yourself, if you're shy), and shake the jar a few times. Reach in and take a heart. Cupid has answered! Pass the jar to a friend and continue taking turns to find out how your romantic future will unfold.

Conversation Heart Cupcake Toppers

Conversation Hearts
Cupcakes, baked and iced

Decorate cupcakes with conversation hearts!

Conversation Heart Cereal Treats

20 large marshmallows

2 tablespoons margarine or butter

3 cups frosted oat cereal with marshmallow bits

12 large conversation hearts

Line an 8- or 9-inch square pan with aluminum foil, leaving 2-inch overhangs on two sides. Generously grease or spray with nonstick cooking spray. Melt the marshmallows and margarine in a medium saucepan over medium heat for 3 minutes or until melted and smooth, stirring constantly. Remove from heat. Add cereal and stir until completely coated.

Spread the mixture in the prepared pan, pressing evenly with a greased rubber spatula. Press heart candies into tops of treats while the treats are still warm, spacing evenly to allow one heart per bar. Let cool 10 minutes. Using foil overhangs as handles to remove treats from pan. Cut into twelve bars.

16

SMS ME

TEXT ME

HOW IS TECHNOLOGY CHANGING VALENTINE'S DAY?

If the previous fifteen chapters were to be summed up in a single sentence, it would probably go something like this: Human beings love to celebrate love—and over the course of a few thousand years we've come up with countless ways to do it. So far we've explored the past and present of Valentine's Day, but what about the holiday's future? With changing times come changing traditions, and nothing in the twenty-first century changes faster than technology.

Technological advances have touched nearly every aspect of our Valentine's Day customs, from the gifts we give to the food we eat, to—perhaps most significantly—the way we express our love. As the popularity of the internet has increased over the past two decades, so has our reliance on it as a way to communicate our every emotion, from mildly intrigued to utterly obsessed. Never has it been easier or faster for the smitten to pursue the object of his or her desire—and never has a suitor had such a variety of tools with which to do it. An infatuated Victorian might while away an hour choosing a Valentine with just the right amount of frill, but that's nothing compared to the seemingly endless selection of e-cards, video cards, links, posts, texts, and tweets modern-day Romeos and Juliets literally have at their fingertips.

While social networking technology has vastly increased the ways in which Valentine's Day sentiments can be shared, it has also given us an equal number of opportunities to turn a budding romance into a bad memory. So fearsome is this paradox that each

February brings with it a new crop of articles touting the appropriate digital romance etiquette (DO text your sweetheart the occasional spontaneous "I love you." DON'T opt for an e-card starring an animated bunch of flowers over a bouquet of actual roses.). Articles also warn of the consequences of failing to turn off one's smart phone on a date, or "friending" a new Valentine too soon. Making pre–Valentine's Day headlines as well are horror stories about how technology has destroyed romance for good. In a survey of more than 2,500 people, for example, the UK's *Telegraph* reported that while more than two-thirds of respondents admitted to having texted "I love you," nearly the same amount had never written an actual pen-and-paper love letter.

Nevertheless, it's impossible to deny that technology has improved Valentine's Day in numerous ways—and promises to continue to do so. Sweethearts forced by circumstances to be separated on February 14 no longer need to make do with saying, "I love you," in words alone. Video communication technology makes it possible for far-flung lovers to share their feelings face-to-face, regardless of the oceans or time zones that separate them. E-commerce Web sites allow us to choose from countless varieties of chocolates and flowers to find the perfect gift for that special someone, and to have it delivered to their doorstep overnight, as long as we're willing to pony up for the postage. Our Valentine's Day celebrations are even poised to benefit from advances in medical and food technology. In 2009, *National Geographic* reported on four new drugs in development that are intended to increase humans' ability to experience love and desire. And new products such as le Whif, a "chocolate inhaler" that allows users to taste the indulgent treat without adding to their waistlines, will surely be welcomed by those who are attempting to "trim the fat" from their Valentine's Day festivities.

What does the next decade, century, or millennium hold for the Day of Love? That, of course, remains to be seen. It's safe to assume, however, that technology will continue to make saying, "I love you," both easier and more complicated every year. Which is to say that everything . . . and nothing . . . will change.

Did You Know?

Welcome to the age of Web-based video valentines. In a study entitled the Future of Video Communications, the Institute for the Future (IFTF) reported that the use of video communication technology such as Skype increases up to 50 percent on major holidays.

When even Hallmark starts selling electronic Valentines, the writing is on the wall (or Blackberry, as it were) for the future of pen-and-paper hearts. With that in mind, Debra Goldstein and Olivia Baniuszewicz, the gals who coined the term flirtexting (and wrote a book about it) have put together some perfect texts for singletons.

1. It's 2/14. Aka Valentine's day. You are single. I am single. Do you see where I'm going with this?

2. Happy Valentine's day. You're so out of everyone's league, I figure you must be home alone. Wanna hang out?

3. Hi. I'd like to forget our awkward first meeting by sending this awkward Valentine's day text. Here goes nothing: Happy Valentine's day!

4. Happy Valentine's day! Did I ignore your first invite? Feel free to try again soon ;).

5. If I don't meet your standards for a Valentine's date, then please lower your standards.

6. [Question] What's worse than a bunch of starry-eyed people-in-love running around? Text back for answer. [Answer] Not being able to see you tonight.

7. Roses are red, violets are blue, we should make out...don't u think so too?

8. Fill in the blank: Valentine's day is a _____ holiday.

For more digital dating tips, buy the book *Flirtexting* and log on to Deb and Liv's Web site, www.flirtexting.com.

Chocolate Mousse in the Raw

For some, the Raw Food movement is the way of the future when it comes to nutrition. Celebrate Valentine's Day the Raw Food way with this sweet treat . . .

2 tbsp coconut cream

2 tbsp cacao powder

1 avocado

2–3 dates

1 cup coconut water or filtered water

1 pinch sea salt

½ tsp vanilla extract

Combine all ingredients in a blender or food processor and blend at high speed until smooth. Serve alone or with your choice of fruit.

Will & Kate

As if a fairytale stepped off the pages of a storybook, the romance between young Prince William and his love Kate Middleton has left the public clamoring to know more about the two picture-perfect royal lovebirds. Catherine Middleton and Prince William, Duke of Cambridge, first met at the University of St. Andrew's in Scotland, in 2001. Ever since, William's royal status has caused almost every aspect of their relationship to be scrutinized and judged by the media, and likewise by people all over the world. The public became very attached to the royal couple as their relationship bloomed and grew. Kate was the archetypal girl-next-door who came from an upper-middle class family and charmed everyone with her down-to-earth attitude. Her poise and clear love for William had citizens of the UK and elsewhere praying for a royal wedding.

Newlyweds Will and Kate

Unfortunately, the public was watching a little too closely, and all of the unwanted media attention caused a temporary split in April, 2007. Kate took this breather as a moment to consider what a life with William would mean. The much-anticipated news came a few months later that the pair had resumed dating, on conditions that the press would back off. A life without William apparently just wasn't an option for Kate. On Nov. 16, 2010, the couple announced their engagement, and the world began preparations for the wedding of the century. Kate wore the same beautiful sapphire ring that William's beloved mother, Princess Diana, wore during her engagement. Does it get any more romantic than that? On April 29, 2011, William and Kate were married. After the ceremony the bride paraded through the city in true princess fashion in a horse drawn carriage, wearing a beautiful gown. Kate's tale of romance made every woman feel that perhaps her dreams too might come true.

Buckingham Palace

17

DATE NIGHT
UNIQUE IDEAS FOR SWEEPING YOUR LOVED ONE OFF THEIR FEET

As society has evolved over the generations, so has courtship. When our grandparents were young, dating was a considerably more formal affair. A girl's parents expected to be formally introduced to a suitor before allowing their daughter to spend time with him. Fast forward a few decades and a hurried, "I'm going out. Don't wait up," is about as much information a parent of teens can hope for today. If dating has lost its ritual, however, it has gained considerable creativity. Dinner and a movie are passé. So is the tradition of the man always paying for the date. Now, there are two extremes: Staying in with a bottle of wine or a sixpack and the remote control, or going out on the town and pulling out all the stops. . .

TEN CRAZY ROMANTIC DATE IDEAS:

1. **Skydiving:** An exhilarating way to quicken the heart, skydiving can make for both a creative date and a great memory—make sure someone documents the occasion! For obvious reasons, this option is probably not one to "surprise" your date with. Confirm beforehand that he or she is excited—not terrified—by the prospect of taking the leap.

2. Go rustic: Being far away from the urban nightlife doesn't mean that you can't go on a great date. Get in touch with your pastoral side and spend an afternoon or a weekend at a working farm. Pick apples together, or feed the livestock—what's cuter than watching your honey get nuzzled by a horse? Go off the beaten path and visit a llama farm—you can even take home some luxurious llama yarn as a souvenir.

3. Try a new sport together: Not feeling basketball? Try something completely new. Get into curling, rock climbing, or even—depending on your location and connections—cheese rolling. Break out the roller skates. Getting active together is an excellent way to bond.

Romantic Movies

- Casablanca
- Love, Actually
- Wall-E
- When Harry Met Sally
- Breakfast at Tiffany's
- Amélie
- Eternal Sunshine of the Spotless Mind
- The Graduate
- You've Got Mail
- Pretty Woman

4. **Build a fort:** Take a break from going out and plan a romantic staycation reliving your favorite childhood activities. Take the sheets and pillows off your bed and make a fort. Toast up some s'mores and make

hot chocolate (feel free to spike it). Turn out the lights, grab your flashlights and have an indoor campout.

5. **Everything new:** Take a page from Holly Go-lightly's book, and spend a day doing things that you've never done be-fore. Take turns. Have you never made a prank call? Now's your chance! Has he never ridden the bus? Treat him to the bus fare and take a ride together. Who knows where you'll end up, but you'll definitely enjoy the ride.

6. **Try an unfamiliar cuisine:** Find the most intriguing restaurant you can—Ethiopian, perhaps? Malagasy?—and settle down a meal neither of you have ever tried. Be daring and don't cheat. If dinner is underwhelming, there's always dessert.

Romantic Songs

- A Kiss To Build a Dream On – Louis Armstrong
- Truly, Madly, Deeply – Savage Garden
- Let's Do It (Let's Fall In Love) – Cole Porter
- That's Amore – Dean Martin
- Eternal Flame – The Bangles
- Lovesong – The Cure
- Your Body Is a Wonderland – John Mayer
- Wouldn't It Be Nice – The Beach Boys
- Ain't No Mountain High Enough – Marvin Gaye and Tammi Terrell
- And I love Her – The Beatles

7. **Improv:** Find a dramatic old movie. Set it on mute and invent your own dialogue together. Give the characters new names, new personalities, even new genders. Get as extreme as you want to—it's your show.

8. **Weekend getaway:** Search a travel site for random, last minute discounted flights and choose a destination neither of you have ever visited. Book an off-the-beaten-path hotel. Pack light. Enjoy being tourists in a place you never expected you'd be going.

9. **Take a class together:** Learn the art of mixing classic cocktails and plan a swanky soiree. Take trapeze lessons, or master skeet shooting. Discover hidden talents, try something you've always wanted to do or make complete fools of yourselves. No matter what happens, you'll end up with great stories to tell.

10. **When in doubt:** Add color to your romantic evening with a theme. Saving up for a tropical vacation? Give your sweetheart a taste of the trip-to-by by draping leis over the furniture and serving iced cocktails with paper umbrellas. Are you both Dickens fans? Dress up in period garb and read aloud from *Great Expectations*. Be sure to gather photographic evidence.

Pick-Up Lines and Compliments

- I bet the sun rises just to see you smile.
- They must have been crazy to let an angel as beautiful as you out of heaven.
- So you must be the reason men fall in love.
- They say the eyes are the mirror to the soul. You have one beautiful soul.
- Hey, don't frown—you never know who might be falling in love with your smile.
- Your eyes are beautiful. You should never shut them, not even at night.
- You look really nice tonight, and I just had to say hello.
- You know, you might be asked to leave soon. You're making all the other women look really bad.
- I'm out of lines at the moment, but if I had one, I'd use it on you.
- *When in doubt*: [smile] Hello.

ABOUT SOME OF THE CARDS FEATURED IN THIS BOOK

Several of the vintage cards pictured in *Valentine Miscellany* were actual cards received by the editor's great-grandmother. They were kept in an old bureau, and discovered by chance soon before this book went to press. The cards are from the early 1900s. They are from the collection of Irene Skidmore.

Those particular illustrations appear on the following pages: 74, 90, 91, 94, 95, 100, 134.

Other cards came from the extensive collection of Nancy Rosen, including those featured on pages 108 and 109. For more information, please go to her website, www.victoriantreasury.com .

Pg 31, Courtesy of Ever Jean/Shutterstock.com

Pg 156, Courtesy of Maria Gioberti/Shutterstock.com

Pg 162, Courtesy of Veloral/Shutterstock.com

Unless otherwise photographs are licensed by Shutterstock.com or Wikimedia Commons.